Alive
and Well

Alive and Well

A Study of the Church

1 JOHN

RANDAL EARL DENNY

Beacon Hill Press of Kansas City
Kansas City, Missouri

To Ruth,
Shannon, and Shelley,
who love me in spite of myself

Contents

Acknowledgments

Preaching from the Word of God is a high privilege. Though I don't know why God called me for that assignment, it is my great adventure week by week. To God I am grateful.

Appreciation is hereby expressed for permission to quote from copyrighted material as follows:

Chosen Books: Charles W. Colson, *Born Again.*

Impact Books, a division of John T. Benson Publishing Company: Reuben Welch, *We Really Do Need Each Other.*

Loizeaux Brothers, Inc.: H. A. Ironside, *Addresses on the Epistles of John and an Exposition of the Epistle of Jude.*

Victor Books, a division of SP Publications, Inc.: Warren W. Wiersbe, *Be Real.*

Westminster Press: William Barclay, *The Letters of John and Jude* in *The Daily Study Bible Series.*

Word Books, Publisher: Ray C. Stedman, *Life by the Son.*

I owe a great debt to my wife, Ruth, who has listened to the same preacher for 30 years, and to my congregation, who inspire me to prepare well Sunday after Sunday.

Preface

During recent decades, the Church of Jesus Christ has been diagnosed as having a terminal illness. Even friends of the Church have written a plethora of books on the Church's ills. Frankly, it was quite refreshing to reread the letters written by the apostle John during the first century of the Christian era. He was realistic enough to know that the Church had some real problems, but with his pen he showed how to keep the Church alive and well. His message needs to be heard in our day. The Church has some problems and more than its share of critics. Yet by the hand of Jesus, we can keep our Church alive and well—and have an exciting time doing it!

In spite of various theories, I found no strong reason to doubt that John the apostle is the author of First, Second, and Third John. He was known as Jesus' Beloved Apostle, the one who leaned on Jesus' chest during that fateful Last Supper in the Upper Room. John may have been a youth during Jesus' ministry, but he was one of the inner circle with the Master. Our first glimpse of young John finds him mending nets—and his lasting ministry is one of mending the fellowship of the Church, repairing damage inflicted on the Church within. As an elder statesman of the Church in Ephesus, John was the last link with Jesus' apostolic band. He left Jerusalem before its destruction in A.D. 70 and may have fled Rome after Paul and Peter were martyred. The seven churches in the Book of Revelation probably were John's circuit of supervision during the last two decades of the first century. John the Elder carried a lot of influence and authority in the Church.

It is interesting that in both 2 John and 3 John, the Beloved Apostle conveys the idea, "I have much to write to you . . . I hope to visit you and talk with you face to face" (2 John 12; cf. 3 John 13). I believe that 1 John is his message, John's written sermon, in which he sets forth his heartfelt, Spirit-anointed address face-to-face with his Christian congregations.

Since chronology is not a strong determinant in the arrangement of books of the Bible, it seems to me that 3 John was written first, 2 John followed to correct a problem created by the first letter, and 1 John was the third letter written—a message referred to in both previous letters, 3 John and 2 John.

First John, taken seriously and applied faithfully, can help keep our Church alive and well in our day. As a parish pastor, I led my people through this exciting New Testament letter. At the conclusion, I understood the sentiment of Dr. T. W. Willingham, who wrote, "'When God and I work together, the end product is not perfect. There will be in it the gold of the divine and the dross of the human.' I have learned to accept the dross; for when I am working with God, there is some gold in it, and I was conscious that we were working together."*

1

To Know God
Is to Live

▽

1 JOHN 1:1-4

△

*F*IRST JOHN WAS written between A.D. 90 and 95. It was probably sent along with, or shortly after, the Gospel of John. First John attempted to apply the truth of the Gospel to the problems existing in the churches.

First John is not typical letter writing in that era. Probably 1 John is a written sermon in which John the Elder preaches to defend the faith.

Dangerous heresies were worming their way into the Church. When John wrote his sermon in Ephesus, Jerusalem had already fallen. Efforts to make the Christian faith into a sect of Judaism had failed. However, attempts were being made to compromise Christianity with pagan thought and "to interpret the new faith as a liberal philosophy."[1] John believed that the worst enemy of the church was within its own gates—people compromising their commitment to Jesus as God's Son.

The prevailing heresy, known as gnosticism, presumed that all material substance is inherently evil. Only the nonphysical or nonmaterial is good. It assumed man had fallen because he was imprisoned in a physical body. Holding the body to be evil and sinful, they concluded that

God could not dwell in a physical body. Therefore, Gnostics did not believe in the incarnation of Jesus as God's Son. Some said that Jesus was only a man. Others insisted that He was not physical, only a phantom.

Beliefs are important because beliefs affect our behavior. Gnostics either became ascetics, punishing their bodies for being sinful—or they became libertines, victimized by unbridled passions and indulgences of the flesh. They thought they could be free from sin only after death.

John's attack follows two basic themes. First, God did come in human flesh in the person of Jesus Christ: "This is how you can recognize the Spirit of God: Every spirit that acknowledges that Jesus Christ has come in the flesh is from God, but every spirit that does not acknowledge Jesus is not from God" (4:2-3). Second, the believer walks in God's light, living in righteousness and love: "This is how we know we are in him: Whoever claims to live in him must walk as Jesus did" (2:5-6).

The Gospel of John was written for the purpose of evangelism: "But these are written *that you may believe* that Jesus is the Christ, the Son of God, and that by believing you may have life in his name" (20:31, italics added). First John was written for the purpose of assurance: "I write these things to you who believe in the name of the Son of God *so that you may know* that you have eternal life" (5:13, italics added).

In one way or another, people in every generation ask, "What must I do to inherit eternal life?" (Luke 18:18). In giving man a spirit, God guaranteed endless existence—but that's not eternal life. Eternal life is a quality of life given here and now by God through Jesus Christ. It is received by faith. God made us in His own image with the capacity to know Him and share His wonderful, abundant life.

Man sinned and messed everything up. But did God

give up on man? No! He cursed the tempter but not the tempted. God began the process of re-creating, so that Adam and Eve could be candidates for restoration. The Bible is the inspired Record of God's plan to restore each of us to a level of life He had planned in the beginning.

God sent His own Son to suffer for our sins in our place. Jesus announced, "I have come that they may have life, and have it to the full" (John 10:10). On the eve of His crucifixion, He prayed for us all: "Now this is eternal life: that they may know you, the only true God, and Jesus Christ, whom you have sent" (17:3).

Russian writer Leo Tolstoy went through a difficult era in his life. In weariness of spirit, he walked through a forest one day and saw a poor farmer sitting on a log and eating his lunch of black bread.

After watching the peasant for a while, Tolstoy said, "My friend, I've been looking for a happy man. I believe I have found him in you." The man's gray hair seemed like a halo around his joyful face. Tolstoy asked, "Where did you find such happiness?"

The farmer replied, "Sir, I found it in the only place where you can ever find it in this troubled world. I found it in God. You find God, sir, and you will be alive and vital and happy!"

Shaking the old workman's hand, Tolstoy promised, "My friend, I will seek after God until I find Him."

After many days, Tolstoy experienced that glorious moment when he completely gave his life to God. And immediately God gave it back to him—but greatly enhanced. He found life pulsating through him—re-created by God from within. A new creature in Christ Jesus! Tolstoy testified, "To know God is to live!" "This is eternal life: that they may know you, the only true God."

Life is a tragedy for the person with plenty to live on

but nothing to live for. Statisticians claim there are 22,000 ways of making a living in the United States. But there's only one way of making a life: "To know God is to live."

How do we get to know God? Through Jesus Christ. He is God's great life given to us. To know Him is to have eternal life. The preface of 1 John opens the door to this eternal life.

I. ETERNAL LIFE IS REVEALED

God's Word of life was not invented by theologians, deduced by philosophers, or evolved by scientists. Eternal life was revealed by God himself as He invaded history. Genesis starts, "In the beginning God created the heavens and the earth" (1:1). The Gospel of John starts, "In the beginning was the Word, and the Word was with God, and the Word was God. He was with God in the beginning" (1:1-2). First John starts with the preface, "That which was from the beginning, which we have heard, which we have seen with our eyes, which we have looked at and our hands have touched—this we proclaim concerning the Word of life. The life appeared; we have seen it and testify to it, and we proclaim to you the eternal life, which was with the Father and has appeared to us" (1:1-2).

What God makes, He fills with wonder and life. At His own initiative, God revealed himself through Jesus Christ. As a little boy said, "Jesus is the best photograph God ever had taken!" God didn't reveal himself to empty space. He appeared to real, live people in Israel. No phantom, He was observed by human senses.

First, God's revelation was *heard*. John and the other apostles had heard Jesus speak. They had listened to His voice and felt the impact of His message. Zedekiah asked the prophet Jeremiah, "Is there any word from the Lord?"

(Jer. 37:17). That's what people need to know. Not opinions, speculations, clever guesses—but does God have a word for us?

Three times in the Gospels God did something like that. Three times God broke in on Jesus' career—at His baptism, at the Mount of Transfiguration, and in the court of the Temple—as if to say, "This is how My life should be lived!"

Second, God's revelation was *seen.* John uses a Greek word describing a careful, deliberate inspection of Jesus. The disciples were left with no doubt about the reality of Christ. John says, "We have seen with our eyes"—meaning to take a long look until one has grasped the significance of that Person. John uses the same word in his Gospel: "We have seen his glory" (1:14). Four times in these first three verses, John emphasizes seeing. Seeing qualifies a person as a witness.

Third, God's revelation was *touched* or handled: "Which we have looked at and our hands have touched." The disciples had touched Jesus many times. After the Resurrection Jesus appeared to them behind locked doors: "They were startled and frightened, thinking they saw a ghost. He said to them, 'Why are you troubled, and why do doubts rise in your minds? Look at my hands and my feet. It is I myself! Touch me and see; a ghost does not have flesh and bones, as you see I have'" (Luke 24:37-39).

When told Jesus had arisen, Thomas couldn't believe it. He had missed the meeting of the disciples. Thomas remarked, "Unless I see the nail marks in his hands and put my finger where the nails were, and put my hand into his side, I will not believe it" (John 20:25).

A week later, Jesus appeared to the disciples and Thomas. Jesus said, "Put your finger here; see my hands. Reach out your hand and put it into my side. Stop doubting and believe" (v. 27).

This personal contact with the risen Lord kindled Thomas' faith, and he fell at Jesus' feet, exclaiming, "My Lord and my God!" (v. 28). That's the first time anyone ever said that. The doubter became the greatest believer of all! Jesus revealed himself to be heard and seen and touched.

John used a word for "touch" meaning to grope or feel after in order to find. It describes the touching done by a person in darkness or by a blind man feeling an object to examine it closely.

Helen Keller asked a friend who had just returned from a walk in the woods what she had observed. The friend replied, "Nothing in particular."

Later, Helen Keller asked, "How was that possible? I, who cannot hear or see, find hundreds of things to interest me through mere touch. I feel the dedicated symmetry of a leaf. I pass my hands lovingly about the rough shaggy bark of a pine. Occasionally, if I am very fortunate, I place my hand gently on a small tree and feel the happy quiver of a bird in full song."

That's how those happy disciples touched Jesus—testing reality. And they felt the quiver of eternal life in full song! "To know God is to live!"

II. ETERNAL LIFE IS PROCLAIMED

John writes, "This we proclaim concerning the Word of life. The life appeared; we have seen it and testify to it, and we proclaim to you the eternal life . . . We proclaim to you what we have seen and heard" (vv. 1-3).

Eternal life is not to be hoarded, but shared; not hidden, but told. John uses two words to describe the telling: "testify" and "proclaim."

First, eternal life is proclaimed by authority of *personal experience:* "testify." The apostles had seen and heard Jesus for themselves. Those early Christians were not guided by the New Testament; they wrote it. It is their testimony of how Christ works in lives day by day. Their testimony has all the excitement of the blind man whom Jesus healed. He confessed there were many things he didn't know, but he did know firsthand one great fact: "One thing I do know. I was blind but now I see!" (John 9:25).

John said they would tell "what we have seen and heard" (v. 3). The Greek perfect tense is used in these statements. The perfect tense indicates something still taking place. What they had seen and heard was still having lasting results. The Holy Spirit continued to make use of the vision and message of Jesus. What they had heard was still ringing in their ears; what they had seen was still the compelling vision before them.

Second, eternal life is proclaimed by authority of *divine commission:* "proclaim!" To proclaim, they must have a commission from the Lord. We do not proclaim on our own authority. The news of eternal life must not be monopolized, but given to the few for the benefit of the many. It must be told.

The basis of proclaiming the Good News is: "What we have heard, what we have seen with our eyes, what we beheld and our hands handled, concerning the Word of life . . . we . . . bear witness and proclaim to you" (vv. 1-2, NASB).

III. ETERNAL LIFE IS SHARED

An important key word of 1 John is introduced: "fellowship" (v. 3). The Greek word *koinōnia* is not easily translated into English. It carries an idea of sharing together, partaking together, having in common. The English word "fellowship" has become diluted in today's usage. "Fellowship" is used to describe just about any type of gathering. It misses the strong emphasis of "partnership." Peter uses a derivative of *koinōnia* to say that we "may *participate in the divine nature*" (2 Pet. 1:4). This partnership is deep and intimate, like that of branches and the vine or the body and its members—a sharing of common life.

First, *our shared life is based on our relationship with the Father:* "And our fellowship is with the Father and with his Son, Jesus Christ" (v. 3). To become a Christian is to become related to God the Father. Jesus is the Bridge Builder uniting us with the Father. Our "communion" or "partnership" with God is only possible through the Holy Spirit. He is God's Agent dwelling within us to affect that relationship. God has filled all the gaps between us with His mercy and love. When we are born again, we have this wonderful fellowship with the Father and with Jesus.

We become children of God. We know to whom we belong. We know where we are going. Our fellowship is with God, and we participate in His nature and in His life. He is our Father. "To know God is to live!"

Second, *our shared life is built in fellowship with God's family:* "We proclaim to you what we have seen and heard, so that you also may have fellowship with us" (v. 3). That we "may have fellowship." John uses the present tense, for this is no momentary partnership but a continuing experience, an everlasting fellowship. We have certainly corrupted our idea of fellowship with God's family. We seem to have the attitude: "I'll have fellowship with God's people when and where and if it suits me!" That insults God's purpose and plan for His Church.

Reuben Welch wrote, "Christians are not brought together because they like each other, but because they share a common life in Jesus and are faced with the task of learning how to love each other as members of the family."[2]

One college student told me, "I am surprised at how easily people leave the fellowship of my church—and over such silly little things." The Father intends for us to have deep and lasting and significant fellowship with His family. Welch added, "The church is not the society of the congenial—it is a fellowship based on common life in Jesus. It is the will of God that the Christian life be lived in . . . a fellowship of the shared life."[3]

As God's family, we need to love and be loved. We need to feel we are worthwhile to ourselves and others. These needs can best be met in the context of God's redeemed people.

John emphasizes more than the fellowship of Christians. He speaks of "Christian fellowship"—this partnership based on our common life in Christ. Too often the church goes only deep enough into fellowship to have superficial social camaraderie instead of spiritual fellowship with the Father and with Jesus. Such an artificial cohesiveness can fall apart over methodology and personality. It has no meaningful depth.

Weddings are interesting. What a varied assortment of guests! Mothers, fathers, sisters and brothers, grandparents, uncles and aunts, friends from school or work, neighbors, on and on. In any other social situation, most of these people would have nothing in common. Many of them do not know each other. Some are young; some are old. Some are rich and others poor—the whole spectrum of society might be represented. Yet, all these differences are lost sight of because of their relationship to the couple getting married. They are brought together because of their love for the bride and groom.

The person of Jesus Christ was the secret of unity in the Early Church. He was the focus of its love. Brought close to Him, they were brought together. Personal differences are unimportant in light of our enthusiasm for Jesus. Only when we lose our enthusiasm for Jesus does our love for each other begin to cool. The shared life is ours to enjoy: "What we have seen and heard we tell you also, so that *you* will *join with us* in the *fellowship* we have with the Father and with His Son Jesus Christ!"

Third, *our shared life results in joy:* "We write this to make our joy complete" (v. 4). Some translations say, "your joy." There's only one letter difference between "our" and "your" in English and Greek. Ancient manuscripts are divided. Here's the spirit of it: "And if you do as I say in this letter, then you, too, will be full of joy, and so will we" (v. 4, TLB). When our fellowship with God and with each other is complete, we experience real joy—a quiet inner excitement with life.

As Warren Wiersbe put it, "Fellowship is Christ's answer to the loneliness of life."[4] Joy is the by-product of fellowship with God and His family. "In thy presence is fulness of joy" (Ps. 16:11, KJV).

One of my favorite songs says:

> *Beautiful life with such a Friend;*
> *Beautiful life that has no end!*
> *Eternal life, eternal joy,*
> *He's my Friend!*
> —Will L. Thompson

To know God is to have eternal life. Eternal life begins now and reaches all the way into God's heaven—but as the cruise ship advertisement claims, "Getting there is half the fun!"

To experience eternal life, we must live in the "now." This wonderful life in Christ is available today. John's Gospel and his sermon, 1 John, are based on three truths:

First, all men need eternal life.

Second, all men may have eternal life.

Third, all men who have eternal life know they have it! "He who has the Son has life" (1 John 5:12).

"To know God is to live!" Do you know Him? Do you know that you have eternal life? You can settle that once and for all.

2

Walking,
Not Talking

▽

1 JOHN 1:5-7

△

JOHN STATED THE purpose of his sermon: "My dear children, I write this to you so that you will not sin" (1 John 2:1). A sinning religion is far from John's message of Jesus' teachings. And yet, much in our lives falls so far short of God's purpose.

In our most honest moments, we know that we have sinned and failed. Our failures break our hearts if we care at all.

John opens this section of the sermon by stating his premise: "This is the message we have heard from him and declare to you: God is light; in him there is no darkness at all" (v. 5). The idea that "God is light" was not new. Centuries earlier, David had sung, "The Lord is my light and my salvation" (Ps. 27:1). A following song of praise rejoices, "For with you is the fountain of life; in your light we see light" (36:9). In the Old Testament God's description as light suggests two things, His revelation and His holiness. John adds, "In him there is no darkness at all." God has no dark spots in His character.

We are influenced by our perception of God's character. John's theme is: "God is light." He perceives God as full of splendor and glory, as self-revealing, as a God of purity and holiness, a God who guides His children. "God is light," and when we stand in His presence He reveals our inner life.

How does a God of light relate to people who live in spiritual, moral, and ethical shadows? Jesus has come to bid all our darkness flee!

I. SIN PROHIBITS FELLOWSHIP

Even Christians may have a problem of relationship with God: "If we claim to have fellowship with him yet walk in the darkness, we lie and do not live by the truth" (v. 6).

Like many people today, Gnostics in John's day thought they could lay claim to being children of God while living like the devil. Fellowship with God cannot be divorced from godly living. One scholar wrote, "We may claim to have a saving knowledge of God; but if our lives show no moral likeness to God, our claim is false."[5] Correctness of doctrine cannot substitute for holy living.

To "walk in darkness" leads to sin. It breaks our fellowship with God. We become incompatible with Him; we and He live in two different worlds.

Ships coming from around the world brought rats to the island Maui. Thriving unchecked on the luscious crops, the rats grew in great numbers.

Someone came up with the idea of importing mongooses from the Orient to kill the rats. The mongooses also thrived in Maui—but had little effect on the rats. It turns out that rats are nocturnal, white mongooses hunt in the daylight. Mongooses prefer light; rats prefer darkness. They live in two different worlds.

Though we claim fellowship with God, if we live in

darkness we are not walking with Him. We cannot *be* righteous without *living* righteously.

What does "darkness" represent in John's mind? The Bible speaks of darkness in four ways.

First, there's the *darkness of man's sinful nature.* You never have to teach anyone to lie or cheat or get angry or be disobedient. It comes quite naturally. You have to train a child away from those tendencies with which we are all born. By nature we are children of darkness. That's why Jesus said, "You must be born again" (John 3:7)—"from above" (JB, Williams).

Second, there's the *willful darkness of rejecting God's light:* "Light has come into the world, but men loved darkness instead of light because their deeds were evil. Everyone who does evil hates the light, and will not come into the light for fear that his deeds will be exposed" (John 3:19-20).

Third, there's *judicial darkness:* "Give glory to the Lord your God before he brings the darkness, before your feet stumble on the darkening hills. You hope for light, but he will turn it to thick darkness" (Jer. 13:16). Does a God of light sometimes cause darkness? Yes, if people deliberately and continually reject His light.

Fourth, there's *eternal darkness.* It is the final result of turning your back to God's light: "For whom blackest darkness has been reserved forever" (Jude 13). That's why God beckons us to himself, for "God is light."

Before a person embarks on a life of sin, he first breaks fellowship with God. He chooses to walk in darkness. "Darkness" stands for the Christless life, the life in opposition to God.

How can that happen to a Christian? How does darkness get into a room? Simply by shutting off the light. Darkness is the absence of light. As Stedman said, "To walk in darkness means to walk as though there [is] no God . . . It is to be a practical atheist . . . We believe there is a God; we know He is there, but we live as though He [does] not exist."[6] We acknowledge God intellectually, but we ignore Him practically. "We do not expose ourselves to Him. That is walking in darkness."[7]

Is it possible for a Christian to walk in darkness? Yes, by turning off God's light. That's the most common reason for weak, powerless, shallow Christians. How do people turn off God's light and walk in darkness?

First, God's light can be turned off by *avoiding church.* Stedman says incisively:

> Some people stop attending church . . . The Word of God . . . proclaimed from a pulpit, is a channel of God's light. The Word itself is [God's] light . . . If we stop coming to church we escape [God's] light . . . We are no longer made uncomfortable by the [preaching of the] Word. We discover that if we stay away we do not experience that pricking of our conscience which the light awakens . . . "Let us consider how to stir up one another to love and good works, *not neglecting to meet together,* as is the habit of some" (Heb. 10:24-25) . . . It is much more comfortable to sit around in . . . old slippers of the flesh and enjoy oneself at home. That is one way to turn off the light.[8]

Second, God's light can be turned off by *avoiding the Bible.* "Another way is to stop reading the Scriptures . . . [Some people] open [their] Bible. They only hear a verse now and then . . . in church or Sunday School, but they seldom open it for themselves. [Beneath] all the excuses . . . — no time, lots of pressures, and so on—there is really a desire to escape [God's] light."[9]

Third, God's light can be turned off by *avoiding an honest look at yourself.* "Perhaps the greatest cause of weakness among evangelical Christians is that we seldom stop to examine ourselves. We never ask ourselves searching and penetrating questions as to where we are in [our] Christian life.

"The Apostle Paul says, 'Examine yourselves, whether you be in the faith.'"[10] It is easier to hide in the darkness than to face the facts that God's light reveals about us.

Fourth, God's light can be turned off by *hiding behind someone.* "You can walk in darkness by comparing yourself with other Christians . . . You can [always] find a favorite person, someone . . . obviously lower on the scale than you are, and what a comfort [that person is]. Anytime you . . . [get] uneasy about your own spiritual condition, remind yourself of him—or her. 'At least I'm better than him.' If you keep this up you can go on for years walking in darkness without [God's] light ever . . . shining on you."[11]

Fifth, God's light can be turned off by *nursing resentments.* "Blame others . . . Blame the church. Blame the Sunday School. Blame the teachers. Blame your father and mother. Blame your children. Blame the boss. Blame the IRS. But never blame yourself!"[12]

Christian, you cannot walk in darkness without feeling guilty. Guilt underlies much depression in Christians. Suppressed guilt creates that long-faced, somber, lackluster attitude so many Christians excuse as being "religious." It's a sorry attempt to punish themselves for not being what they know they should be—for claiming to have fellowship with God but walking in darkness.

Guilt is to the spirit what pain is to the body. Pain notifies you that something is wrong so that you may correct it. Guilt is God's warning light that something is wrong morally or spiritually. Pay attention to it. Don't try to rid yourself of guilt; take care of the broken relationship with God and others.

To walk in the light means to hide nothing. "If we claim to have fellowship with him yet walk in the darkness, we lie and do not live by the truth." Fellowship is the test of truth. If what we do destroys fellowship, it cannot be truth.

Wiersbe illustrated this lesson vividly:

A congregation was singing, as a closing hymn, the familiar song, "For You I Am Praying." The speaker turned to a man on the platform and asked quietly, "For whom are *you* praying?"

The man was stunned. "Why, I guess I'm not praying for anybody. Why do you ask?"

"Well, I just heard you say, 'For you I am praying,' and I thought you meant it," the preacher replied.

"Oh no," said the man. "I'm just singing."

Pious talk! A religion of words! To paraphrase James 1:22, "We should be doers of the Word as well as talkers of the Word." We must *walk* what we *talk.* It is not enough to know the language; we must also live the life. "If we say" [vv. 6, 8, 10, KJV]—then we ought also *to do.*[13]

II. GOD PROMISES RESTORATION
TO FELLOWSHIP

"But if we walk in the light, as he is in the light, we have fellowship with one another" (v. 7).

Our fellowship with God must be more than mere "talk"; we must also "walk." God's promise to restore our fellowship is conditional: "But if . . ." Fellowship is not guaranteed. It is conditioned on our willingness to "walk in the light, as he is in the light."

First John 1:6-7, 8-9, and 10—2:2 are three couplets. Each follows a similar idea and expression of thought. Each couplet begins with "if." Dr. Willingham noted, "The challenge of the *ifs* can be measured only by the grandeur of the promises that follow them."[14] In this first couplet, verses 6-7, the promise of restoration is fellowship with God the Father.

"But if we *walk* in the light." The Greek word for "walk" appears in a second-century manuscript in the sentence: "I am *going about* in a disgraceful state." That word "going about" or "walk" refers to conduct—one's thoughts, words, and deeds! The grammar indicates continuous action: "If we are constantly walking or going about in the light." There's no Sunday religion here. Walking in light is the normal experience of a Christian who lives according to God's Word. John's advice is to "keep on walking in the light." This continual "walking" in the Lord's presence suggests progress in the Christian life. God intends for us to make spiritual advancement. If you are still the spiritual infant you were 1 or 5 or 10 years ago, you have not been walking in God's light. You've been talking, not walking.

One writer pointed out, "It does not say if we walk *according* to light, but it says, 'if we walk *in* the light.' It is *where* you walk, not *how* you walk. It is to walk in the presence of God."[15] That means going where God leads you; that means growing where God feeds you; that means overflowing where God needs you!

Nelda Bishop Reed told of a potted plant that leaned from her desk at about 30 degrees toward the sunlight shining through the window. When she turned it around, it was soon tilting toward the light again. She said, "If I were only attracted as irreversibly toward God's love and delight! Today, I want . . . to bring my heart in tune with God and to revel in His glory. Like my plant, I want to bend my life to receive more light from Him.

"I need that kind of persistence! When the devil turns me around and tries to discourage me, I want to lean toward the Light."[16]

Jesus Christ is Victor over the world's darkness. Darkness cannot extinguish light! If we learn to walk in honesty and openness with Christ, we can enjoy His guidance. The quality of our response depends on our motivation. Some people obey because they *have* to, some because they *need* to, but others because they *want* to. The way of light is the way of delight: "for the joy of the Lord is your strength" (Neh. 8:10).

As God's light falls on us, it may reveal spots and blemishes—even sins—that need to be corrected. We can refuse to accept the disclosure, try to cover it over, or pretend we don't see it. That attitude will lead us into willful sin. Or we can accept what God shows us, thank Him for being faithful to reveal our need, and embrace His provision for our restoration—without any loss of righteousness before the Lord. He will make a way for us.

"But if we walk in the light, as he is in the light, we have fellowship with one another." Our fellowship is based on a life shared with Christ as a result of our new birth. Since we have this deep, intimate partnership with God, we will have common likes and dislikes with Jesus. What our Lord loves, we will learn to love. What He hates, we will learn to hate.

John describes this fellowship "with one another" by using a pronoun in the Greek text that means giving and returning mutual love to each other. This reciprocal love is twofold. When something hinders one fellowship, it hinders the other. If I get out of sorts with the Lord, it affects my relationship to others. If I get out of sorts with God's people, it affects my fellowship with Christ.

Someone may say, "I have difficulty having fellowship with Christ. John and the apostles had an advantage. They lived when Jesus walked on earth. They knew Jesus personally. I was born 20 centuries too late!"

That's wrong. It was not the apostles' *physical* nearness to Jesus that made the difference. It was their *spiritual* nearness. "They had committed themselves to Him as . . . Savior and . . . Lord. Jesus Christ was real and exciting to John and his colleagues because they had trusted Him. By trusting Christ, they had *experienced eternal life.*"[17]

The only way any of us can enter into fellowship with Jesus is by trusting Him, betting our lives on Jesus Christ and the integrity of God's promise of restoration.

III. JESUS PROVIDES CLEANSING FOR FELLOWSHIP

John wrote, "And the blood of Jesus, his Son, purifies us from all sin" (v. 7).

"The blood of Jesus" symbolizes the whole life of Jesus Christ, freely given and poured out at the Cross to redeem this old broken world. Calvary was God's act of giving up life in order to give us new life. In Jesus, God became a man uniting himself with us in our finite experience. In creation, man was made in the image of God. In the Incarnation, God took on the image of man. God revealed himself in human experience, suffered for the sins of the world, and by the power of the Resurrection life gave us hope beyond ourselves. Jesus Christ is our provision of righteousness.

How does that happen? "And the blood of Jesus, his Son, purifies us from all sin." That word "purifies" or "cleanseth" (KJV) is in the present tense, suggesting that His blood is continually cleansing as we walk in His light. While our cleansing begins in a crisis moment, we are kept in a purifying process as we maintain contact with our Lord. One writer put it, "Our being kept cleansed is conditioned upon our continuing to 'walk in the light.'"[18]

If you are walking with Jesus Christ, His cleansing work is in progress at this moment. By hearing and reading God's Word, we can allow the Holy Spirit to work in our hearts and minds, chipping away imperfections and blemishes that He wants to remove. He brings to our attention what we need to admit and confess and yield to Him. Moment by moment, He is at work, purifying our hearts by faith. The cleansed life is not living to the best of our abilities or trying harder. It is living and trusting in Christ's ability. In Him we are kept pure and holy.

Here's good news: "All sin" is included. Nothing in our past is too great for God. We don't have to justify ourselves; Christ alone can justify us. The blood of Jesus Christ can't cleanse excuses, but it can cleanse every confessed sin! Jesus said, "I have come into the world as a light, so that no one who believes in me should stay in darkness" (John 12:46).

Make that continual prayer of openness before God: "Search me, O God, and know my heart; test my thoughts. Point out anything you find in me that makes you sad, and lead me along the path of everlasting life" (Ps. 139:23-24, TLB).

If unconfessed sin has hindered your fellowship with Christ or another person, come to the Lord now for His cleansing. If you have failed to follow the light God has given you, come to Him now. If there are unyielded areas of your life that God has revealed to you, come to Him now. "But if we walk in the light, as he is in the light, we have fellowship with one another, and the blood of Jesus, his Son, purifies us from all sin."

> *Out of my bondage, sorrow, and night,*
> *Jesus, I come; Jesus, I come.*
> *Into Thy freedom, gladness, and light,*
> *Jesus, I come to Thee.*
> —William T. Sleeper

3

Washed White, Not Whitewashed

▽

1 JOHN 1:8-9

△

*T*HE APPLICATION FOR a new driver's license had the question: "Have you ever been arrested?"

The applicant put down, "No."

The next question was: "Why?"

The applicant wrote: "Never been caught."

That's the oft-accepted attitude toward sin today. It's only wrong if you get caught. Such a concept of morality deals with sin as something outside of the real "me."

The real problem of sin is not its expressions (acts of sin) but its source (the rebellious spirit). Henry David Thoreau said, "There are a thousand hacking at the branches of evil to one who is striking at the root." Policemen, sheriffs, lawyers, judges, juries, lawmakers, and often doctors are exhausted from hacking at the acts of sin. They try to curb the "unacceptable sins" of society. But God's Word strikes at the root—a cure for the carnal nature, that sinful spirit of rebellion against God.

Columnist William Miller wrote in the *New York Times*: "We have violence in our streets because there is violence in our hearts."

The old humanistic liberalism has collapsed out of

frustration and failure. Putting a person in a good environment has not made him good. Social evolution, ignoring the problem of sin, went backward. Giving money to the poor did not cure their poverty. It only postponed the day of responsible action.

Holy Scripture gives the only answer that works. Humanistic efforts to change man's carnal nature end in bitter disappointment. People attempt to whitewash sin; God's way is to wash white: "'Come now, let us reason together,' says the Lord. 'Though your sins are like scarlet, they shall be as white as snow; though they are red as crimson, they shall be like wool'" (Isa. 1:18).

King David, a man after God's own heart, slipped into sin. After that tragic fall, Nathan the prophet confronted David with his sin. Psalm 51 is David's prayer for forgiveness of sins, for cleansing of a rebellious nature, and for restoration to God's family and fellowship.

> O loving and kind God, have mercy. Have pity upon me and take away the awful stain of my transgressions. Oh, wash me, cleanse me from this guilt. Let me be pure again. . . . I was born a sinner, yes, from the moment my mother conceived me. You deserve honesty from the heart; yes, utter sincerity and truthfulness. . . .

> Sprinkle me with the cleansing blood and I shall be clean again. Wash me and I shall be whiter than snow. . . . Create in me a new, clean heart, O God, filled with clean thoughts and right desires. . . . Restore to me again the joy of your salvation, and make me willing to obey you *(vv. 1-2, 5-7, 10, 12, TLB)*.

God's solution is not covering over, but cleansing. Instead of spanking your hand for an act of sin, God would create in you "a new, clean heart, . . . filled with clean thoughts and right desires."

John wrote: "If we claim to be without sin, we deceive ourselves and the truth is not in us. If we confess our sins, he is faithful and just and will forgive us our sins and purify us from all unrighteousness" (vv. 8-9). John digs deeper than our acts of sin. He deals with the carnal sin nature. Sin is not a "thing," but an attitude hindering our relationship with God.

I. SIN HINDERS FELLOWSHIP

"If we claim to be without sin, we deceive ourselves and the truth is not in us" (v. 8).

That's a fascinating claim: "If we claim to be without sin." In verses 6 and 7, the first couplet lays bare the problem of fellowship with God. John says that failure to admit one's inner rebellion brings a rift into our fellowship with God.

In his graphic way, Reuben Welch says:

> Some groups use the word "sin," for anything short of the divine ideal, whether it is a bad mood in the morning or shooting your grandmother at night. And some people just don't use the word "sin" at all in connection with Christian people in the church. You say "sin" and they immediately think of the bad guys on the outside . . . I . . . use the word "failure." Maybe then, we won't be so tempted to pass this section of 1 John on to others who need it. We "all" need it.[19]

Ray Stedman sensed the same capacity for excusing sin: "The fancier the name the more we like it, because it sounds so much better than that simple, ugly, three-letter word, sin . . . The evil twist of our fallen nature is revealed in the fact that what others do we call sin, but when we do the same things, we have a different name for it . . . As long as we can find a nicer label we will never treat the thing like the poison it is."[20]

"If we claim to be without sin." John is talking about the "sin principle," which is eventually expressed by acts of sin. Though we have entered into eternal life by the free gift of grace, we soon discover a principle of sin deep in our hearts. John wants to confront us with that reality. First, *some people won't face sin.* They deny that sin exists in their hearts. They will insist, "I could never do a thing like that!" Thus, God's cleansing is refused.

Second, *some people deny the fact of sin.* Swept up in modern mores of a Freudian value system, they believe sin doesn't exist. Therefore, no one is actually a sinner. If it feels good, it must be good. Or having come to Jesus for forgiveness of past sinful acts, they are ignorant of the hidden sin nature that remains. Thus, God's cleansing is ignored.

Third, *some people simply refuse responsibility for sin.* So long as sin is looked upon as a weakness, a disease, a result of heredity or environment, it is simply one's fate—but not his fault. Again, God's cleansing is not accepted.

Fourth, *some people remain naive about sin.* They say, "I'm saved; my sins are forgiven—past, present, and future. Therefore, I have no need for additional light from God because I cannot lose out spiritually. I shall go right on living as I wish." So, God's cleansing is rejected.

The Bible affirms, "If we claim to be without sin, we deceive ourselves." If we say we have no capacity to sin, we are deceiving ourselves—literally, leading ourselves astray.

The *National Geographic* magazine had an article about American bison, known popularly as "buffalo." The author told how big and powerful buffalo are. Careful protection has helped them back from the edge of extinction. In fact, proper herd management has made it necessary to sell surplus animals. A ranger recalled experiences with uninformed buyers who came to purchase surplus buffalo: "One lady showed up with a leash to claim hers. She took one look and went home empty-handed."[21]

That's how successful we are with self-help methods

of taming sin. We attempt to lead around something we can't handle. "We deceive ourselves."

John wrote to people, then and now, who were deceived into thinking they could have fellowship with God while they practiced sin. It wouldn't work then, and it doesn't work now.

Regardless of reformations and resolutions to safeguard our actions, John tells us the great problem is our sinful nature that raises its ugly head in rebellion, destroying fellowship with God.

"If we claim to be without sin, we deceive ourselves and the truth is not in us." Only by admitting sin can we surrender it to the Lord and receive His cleansing. If our sin nature remains unconfessed and uncleansed, "the truth is not in us."

The old sin nature, though hidden for a while, is always revealed. Truth always wins. "If we refuse to admit that we are sinners, then we live in a world of illusion and truth becomes a stranger to us" (v. 8, Phillips).

Our sin nature hinders all our relationships.

II. GOD PROMISES RESTORATION

Disrupted relationships? Yes, but "if we confess our sins, he is faithful and just and will forgive us our sins" (v. 9). Sins are the inevitable results and expressions of a sin nature.

"If we confess our sins." The word "confess" literally means "to say the same thing." To confess my sins means to say the same thing about them that God says about them. He calls them "sins" and tells me I am responsible for them. Confession means I agree with Him. God is absolutely right about me.

A counselor tried to help a man who had come forward during an evangelistic invitation. The man told the counselor, "I'm a Christian, but there's sin in my life. I need help."

The counselor showed him 1 John 1:9 and suggested that he confess his sins to God.

The man began praying, "O Father, if we have done anything wrong—"

The counselor interrupted. "Just a minute. Don't drag *me* into your sin! My brother, it's not 'if' or 'we'—you'd better get down to business with God!"

Confession is agreeing with God that I have sin in my life—not "if" and not "we."

John put the word "confess" in a present, active tense, meaning "if we keep on confessing." As we go, we keep on confessing. Confession is the first human step toward restoring our fellowship with God. God has already promised restoration.

At the heart of confession is the intent to forsake our sins—to turn away from them and turn toward God for life and help. We'll not be forgiven for sins we don't sincerely intend to quit. "If we keep on confessing" and forsaking known sin, we'll never develop the habit pattern of deliberately sinning and walking in darkness. God has promised restoration through Jesus, our great High Priest, who "is able to be saving completely . . . being always alive for . . . continually making intercession for them" (Heb. 7:25, Wuest).

Our sins become the circuit breaker in our relationship with God and cast us into the darkness described in verse 7. The Bible makes it clear that a break in fellowship always comes from our side—never God's. But He has promised to restore our relationship with Him. As we confess our sins, He takes the broken ends of fellowship and unites us with himself. Once again His power and blessing flow through us.

"If we confess our sins, he is faithful and just" (v. 9).

The Lord is faithful to forgive sins when we confess them to Him. His forgiveness is dependable: "I will forgive and forget their sins" (Jer. 31:34, TLB). Satan only comes to accuse; God reveals our sins so that we might confess them to Him. God knows we have feet of clay, that we have His treasure in earthen jugs! (See 2 Cor. 4:7.) There's no need for despair and discouragement when God brings our sins to consciousness. Simply confess them and agree with God that they are sin. Then take His release and freedom!

God brings guilt to His children only for correction—not condemnation. Matthew Arnold described it:

> He took the suffering human race,
>   He read each wound, each weakness clear—
> And struck His finger on the place
>   And said—"Thou ailest here, and here."

God reveals in order to heal our broken fellowship with Him. Someone said, "The holiness of God excuses no sin, but the love of God forgives all sin through Christ."

Sin comes between us and God's greatest gift, Jesus Christ. But, wonder of wonders, sin can be removed through Christ's atoning blood, so that there's nothing between us and God's wonderful Gift! Jesus makes God accessible to us.

"He is faithful and just and will forgive us our sins." Dr. H. Orton Wiley said, "With one arm, Jesus reaches into the loving heart of the Father and with the other He reaches into the broken heart of a lost humanity and in Himself He brings the two together."[22]

III. JESUS PROVIDES CLEANSING

"He is faithful and just and will forgive us our sins and purify us from all unrighteousness" (v. 9).

An act of sin is something we can control, but the fact of sin in our nature controls us. For the acts of sin, John prescribes God's forgiveness. For the fact of sin, the tendency to rebel, John tells of God's cleansing. "He . . . will forgive us our sins and purify us from all unrighteousness." The word "purify" or "cleanse" (KJV) in this verse is in the Greek aorist tense, indicating a completed action. It is the "all at once" cleansing of sanctification. There's no gradual cleansing from impurity of heart, but an act of God's grace once for all.

No amount of fixing up can change man's inner nature or gradually make it better. Trying to whitewash over hidden sin only makes it dirtier than ever. A transformation is needed—a divinely changed nature, a thorough cleansing by God that makes the heart "whiter than snow."

The biblical word for this transformation of the inner nature is sanctification: "This is the will of God, even your sanctification" (1 Thess. 4:3, KJV). Jesus leads the believers into "a deeper relationship with Him through the experience of 'entire sanctification.'"[23] The Holy Spirit who is resident in you becomes President in you.

The cleansed, pure life is characterized by openness, honesty, and confession. Instead of boasting in our progress, we become more sensitive to God's voice and ready to admit sin and seek cleansing. Jesus desires to "purify us from *all* unrighteousness."

Missionary Eunice Bryant wrote, "Often I have worked with friends who have sought divine forgiveness without full repentance. One wanted God to cure his alcoholism but let him continue living in adultery . . . But God's laws do not bend to fit our compromises. Genuine and total repentance brings the joyful witness of the Spirit that all our sins are forgiven." In the same way, Jesus' cleansing is *only* for "*all* unrighteousness"—never partial.

During the Last Supper, Jesus took a towel and a basin of water and went around to all His guests and washed their feet. When He came to Peter, the disciple replied, "No . . . you shall never wash my feet."

Jesus looked at His impetuous, well-meaning friend and said, "Unless I wash you, you have no part with me" (John 13:8). Stedman noted, "I do not mind living with someone who knows his feet get dirty and who . . . frequently washes them, but it is terribly distressing to live with someone who thinks his feet never get dirty. That is what John is saying. If we say we cannot get dirty feet, we deceive ourselves and the truth is not in us."[24]

The sanctified Christian experiences once-for-all cleansing of the heart. However, along the way, walking in a fallen, degrading world, we must be quick to admit whatever "dirt" God shows us. Then we receive His ongoing cleansing as we continue walking in the light with Him.

When we trustfully surrender to Jesus, He forgives all sins and cleanses us from all unrighteousness. Sin is removed. The taint is gone. The heart is made pure, filled with His Spirit. But we need the daily application of the Cross to enable us to walk "in the light, as he is in the light" (v. 7). The Holy Spirit keeps on working in us as we respond to Him.

Writing that we sin not, John advertises the blood of Christ as God's perfect antidote for all unrighteousness—both the acts of sin and the fact of inner sin. Jesus is God's provision for our sin problem, restoring us to fellowship. It makes me feel like echoing the bumper sticker that proclaimed: "God Said It—I Believe It—and That Settles It."

Whatever God shows me, I want to take care of right now. I want to keep short accounts with Him. The test of my sanctification is the length of time it takes me to get to the Cross when God shows me something to be confessed and corrected.

Frankly, I want God's judgment now—not later—so I can admit He is right, and so He can take care of it now! Thank God, we can deal with the problem of sin at this very moment and strike it at its root. We don't have to wait for a thing. God reveals our sin, and He reveals His adequacy of grace to cleanse us from sin. Don't try to whitewash over sin in your life, but bring it to Him and let Him wash you whiter than snow!

4

Stumbling, Not Stopping

▽

1 JOHN 1:10—2:2

△

*T*HE MORE WE walk with Jesus, the less likely we are to stumble. But if we do stumble, it is important to run at once to Him for cleansing. "If any man sin, we have an advocate with the Father, Jesus Christ the righteous" (1 John 2:1, KJV).

The church is not a showcase for saints posed in finished perfection. Honestly, we ought to hang out a warning sign: "Danger! Saints Under Construction."

Construction involves risk. Opportunities for success imply possibilities of failure. Every church is saddened when someone within its fellowship falls away from Jesus. But I have never known a person to fall away who was doing everything he could to keep from it.

In an editorial, William McCumber asked, "What can be done to prevent backsliding?" He suggested keeping a faithful devotional life. Almost without exception, backsliders have confessed their neglect of God's Word and prayer. If you expect to be an Olympic champion, you can't neglect nutrition, water, and exercise. And don't expect to be strong spiritually if you neglect the Bible and prayer. "A Christian without devotions is like Popeye without spinach, no match for [life's] pressures and problems." Apart from Jesus, we have no abiding strength. McCumber concluded, "The best way to keep from backsliding is to see how close to God you can live, not how near the world you can survive."[25]

Some people around the churches of John's day had been spreading the false idea that a Christian can freely practice sin. John responds with his sermon: "so that you will not sin" (2:1). Even today many people take backsliding lightly. My heart breaks over people who say, "Yes, I'm a Christian. I was baptized as a baby." Or, "I'm a Christian because I made a decision for Jesus years ago." Yet their lives contradict their claims. John says, "This is how we know we are in him: Whoever claims to live in him must walk as Jesus did" (1 John 2:5-6).

People trusting in a past relationship with Jesus, yet living in sin, remind me of a prospector whose body was found in the California desert. Apparently he died of thirst, clutching a bag of copper pyrites, "fool's gold." On a piece of paper he had scrawled: "I died rich."

Many people embrace the notion that if we are predestined to go to heaven, we're going whether we sin or not. It's a bag of fool's gold. "No one who lives in him keeps on sinning. No one who continues to sin has either seen him or known him" (1 John 3:6).

The man whose claims are contradicted by his life is a liar.

In the third couplet, 1 John 1:10—2:2, John turns his concern to the person who loves Jesus but who sorrowfully has stumbled spiritually.

The person who stumbles spiritually should not go back and start the race all over again. He should not give up and quit altogether. He should get up and keep on reaching for the high calling of God in Christ Jesus. While

God makes no allowance for sin in the believer, He does make provision for sin.

I. SIN AFFECTS RELATIONSHIPS

"If we claim we have not sinned, we make him out to be a liar and his word has no place in our lives" (v. 10).

Sin is not just the glaring evil that makes newspaper headlines. Sin is anything that hinders our fellowship with Jesus Christ. The most common New Testament word for sin is *hamartia*—missing the target. At whatever point our conduct misses the mark, we must admit hindrance in our love for and fellowship with God. We cannot have fellowship with Him on cheap and easy terms.

How does John define sin? "Sin is lawlessness" (1 John 3:4). Lawlessness pushes beyond God's limits of conduct. It knowingly violates His moral law. I may rationalize, but when God calls an act "sin," I must admit it. Some people excuse sin by suggesting, "Sin is deliberate and willful—but I can't help myself. Therefore, I have not sinned."

Having stumbled, we have a tendency to lie there and argue over who tripped us. The worst excuse says: "It's Your fault, God, not mine. These circumstances that You've allowed . . . make it impossible for me to obey You. Therefore, You're to blame. I want to [obey] . . . I really want to be what I ought to be, but because of these circumstances I can't, so, [God,] it's really Your fault."[26]

John responds, "We make him out to be a liar." The Bible warns, "So, if you think you are standing firm, be careful that you don't fall! No temptation has seized you except what is common to man. And God is faithful; he will not let you be tempted beyond what you can bear. But when you are tempted, he will also provide a way out so

46

that you can stand up under it" (1 Cor. 10:12-13). The devil would have us believe that sin is the final word.

In the early years of our nation, there was no braver soldier than Benedict Arnold. He was a distinguished fighter at Quebec and during many battles of the Revolutionary War. But a single act of treason annulled his record. In West Point Military Academy his picture hangs with its face toward the wall.

When a believer stumbles and sins, Satan desires to leave him with his face turned away from God's fellowship. But John tells us that though a Christian may stumble, he doesn't have to stop there!

II. GOD PROMISES RESTORATION

Some people ask, "Can Christians keep from sinning?" The right question is: "Can the devil get us into a condition that God cannot undo?" "My dear children, I write this to you so that you will not sin. But if anybody does sin, we have one who speaks to the Father in our defense" (2:1).

John's purpose is to prevent sin, not condone it: "so that you will not sin." The grammar suggests, "so that you sin not at all." What God commands, He enables. The glory of God's grace is in the Good News: "It is possible *not* to sin." "I write this to you so that you will not sin. But if anybody does sin . . ." The possibility of sin in the believer is followed immediately by the remedy for sin.

"But if any man sin" (KJV). The Greek tense suggests sin as a definite failure, not an ongoing practice. Some mistakenly believe that a single sin severs the bonds of love between the believer and Christ. That caricatures God as fickle. One writer noted, "To assume that grace is immediately withdrawn from the Christian who sins is to deny the

. . . meaning of grace. If grace is not for sinners, it is not *grace*. If mercy is not for the undeserving, it is not *mercy*. Thank God, grace is for *sinners*, not the sinless—of whom there is none [except] Jesus . . . On-again, off-again 'Christians' who receive so much, and lose it so soon, are a reproach to Christ and His saving grace."[27]

God will reprove and chasten His child for sin, but not disinherit him. Only one's *continued* personal rebellion can annul the effects of grace. I'm so glad that while God makes no allowance for sin, He has made provision for it.

My mother loves to play the piano. The older she gets, the more practice she gets. The more she practices, the more creative she becomes. Mom has developed some beautiful and intriguing piano medley arrangements. I'm quite proud of her work.

However, one thing about her playing drove Dad and me to distraction. When Mom hits a wrong note, she stops and starts over. She may be well into a beautiful song with deep feeling, but no matter how small the mistake, she backs up and starts over.

That's the tragic way many people live their spiritual pilgrimage. One stumble, and they go back and start over at the next revival meeting or youth camp or some overwhelming tragedy—always starting over again with God. I like Reuben Welch's statement: "God's intention for me is to keep going on and not start over at every point of failure. The point of failure should become the occasion for immediate confession and trust in the forgiveness and cleansing of God."[28] He added: "I already know the first five bars of the Christian life by heart. God knows I have played them enough. I've made up my mind to finish the song. I probably couldn't do a perfect performance if I did it a hundred times—and neither can you."[29]

Jesus clearly commands, "Go now and leave your life

of sin" (John 8:11). But how wonderful that God's Word adds, "But if anybody does sin . . ." God knows our weaknesses and has made provision for our stumblings. Instead of covering over our sin, we can confess it immediately and conquer it through Jesus. God intends for us to live victoriously over sin.

God does not intend for us to live in crippling, fearful fellowship with Jesus. God's love frees us, and freedom implies possibility of failure. If we should sin, He has an immediate solution. He picks up the stumbling friend of Jesus and sets him on his way again. Knowing he is loved and has undeserved forgiveness available makes the believer eager to please God, not anxious to avoid Him.

God may be disappointed when we stumble, but not shocked. "If any man sin, we have an advocate with the Father" (2:1, KJV). God has promised restoration. What a healing word: "We have an advocate." At our point of failure, Jesus our Advocate stands by our side and is on our side.[30] He "speaks to the Father in our defense" (2:1).

Our Advocate pleads our cause—and He still pleads for us today. The word "Advocate" stands as opposite to the word "accuser." We need a great Advocate because we have a tough adversary. Satan is "the accuser of our brothers, who accuses them before our God day and night" (Rev. 12:10).

The Bible says, "Who is he that condemns? Christ Jesus, who died—more than that, who was raised to life—is at the right hand of God and is also interceding for us" (Rom. 8:34). When Satan accuses, Jesus our Advocate holds up His nail-scarred hands: "My Father, I took all that into account when I died on the Cross." "He is able to save completely those who come to God through him, because he always lives to intercede for them" (Heb. 7:25).

John says, "We have [present tense, constantly] an advocate." As we go, Jesus is pleading our case at God's throne. The very moment I fail, Jesus takes up my case—even before I am convicted over it. As quickly as Satan would accuse, Jesus represents me. He applies God's Word to my conscience. I feel troubled about my failure and begin confessing it to God. Sometimes it's so subtle that I cry, "Search me, O God, and know my heart: try me, and know my thoughts" (Ps. 139:23, KJV). The Spirit of God probes, "Don't you remember that hasty word, that unholy thought, that crooked thing, that unforgiving spirit?" As I confess my failures, my weaknesses, my sins, I experience God's blessing: "If we confess our sins, he is faithful and just to forgive us our sins, and to cleanse us from all unrighteousness" (1:9, KJV).[31]

All of this has happened, and I'm still a child of God, and I'm continuing in His fellowship. God isn't fickle. I've only stumbled; I did not stop or quit. I have not been disqualified from the race. The work of Jesus Christ brings restoration.

III. JESUS PROVIDES RIGHTEOUSNESS

"Jesus Christ, the Righteous One. He is the atoning sacrifice for our sins, and not only for ours but also for the sins of the whole world" (2:1-2).

Jesus is God's provision for our sin. Our Advocate is available and adequate. His goodness meets the law's requirements.

Two men met in a court of justice; one on the bench and the other before the bar. Though boyhood friends, the judge was duty-bound to hand out the sentence. Justice must be done. After the judge pronounced sentence, he stepped down from the bench, stood beside the prisoner, paid his fine, and said, "Come on, John. Let's go home for dinner!"

That's what Jesus has done for me. He is my Friend, even though He is Judge. By His grace I can feast in His presence. He didn't gloss over my sin, but He himself paid it in full. Jesus is my Righteousness.

In pagan rituals, people brought sacrifices for sins to placate angry gods. In Christianity, we have nothing of merit to bring. The Good News is that God himself has taken the initiative and made the sacrifice for us. He offers himself to satisfy moral justice. We take Him by faith. "God . . . reconciled us to himself through Christ . . . God made him who had no sin to be sin for us, so that in him we might become the righteousness of God" (2 Cor. 5:18, 21).

The Bible says, "Stay away from sin. But if you sin, there is someone to plead for you before the Father" (2:1, TLB). Jesus is God's provision for our righteousness in case we sin.

An ocean liner doesn't leave harbor expecting to founder. As W. T. Purkiser wrote, "No one expects it to sink 'every day in word, thought, and deed.' . . . But it carries a full complement of lifeboats just the same."[32]

Every car runs on four tires. We don't expect flat tires, yet nearly every car has a spare tire. We make provision for the exceptions, the unexpected. If we have provided for a flat, we need only have a momentary interruption to get fixed up to run again.

If a Christian sins, he can barge ahead on his own strength and pretend there's no problem. But, like that flat tire, things get worse. How much better it is to deal with the problem immediately. Quit rationalizing or covering up. When you stumble, confess it, renounce it, and accept the advocacy of Jesus Christ. Keep on going with only momentary interruption. God has provided Jesus for the unexpected and the exceptions that break our hearts. As Dr.

Purkiser noted, "A Christian need never fall, but if he does, he may rise again—sadder but wiser, having discovered at least one point where [he needs to be on guard]."[33]

Yes, I might stumble. What I do about it depends on my determination to reach my destination. If it doesn't matter much to me, I'll just turn around and go back. If I am determined to reach my goal, I'll get up, get things straightened out, and continue walking with Jesus.

Missionary Ruth Blowers was teaching Sunday School children how to pray if they had told a lie or done something wrong. Phrase by phrase, she prayed, and the children followed. As they finished the "Amen," a second grader exclaimed, "Boy, do I feel good!" And why not? Stumbling isn't the final word. The Bible tells us what to do if we stumble.

First, *don't minimize the sin.* Without making excuses, recognize it as sin and admit it to God. Be honest with God—don't call your sin nice names or deceive yourself into thinking your sin is justified.

Second, *accept God's forgiveness.* Quit brooding over sin. Forget it and press on. When the adversary sows doubt, remember you have a great Advocate.

Third, *claim God's cure.* He can keep you from falling. "He breaks the power of canceled sin." Accept God's enabling power through the Holy Spirit. Listen to Jesus and do what He says. If you have fallen, fall on your knees. If you have stumbled, stumble into the arms of Jesus!

5

What You See
Is What You've Got

▽

1 JOHN 2:3-11

△

*A*UGUSTINE PRAYED, "THOU hast made us for Thyself, O Lord, and our hearts are restless until they rest in Thee."[34] But how can I know I know God?

In the apostle John's latter days, Gnostics taught that knowledge is the answer. Convinced that knowledge alone redeemed a person, they lived immoral lives. Believing everything physical was evil, nothing could be done about immorality in this life. So-called illuminated ones disregarded moral law; thus they were no different from pagans. Intellectual knowledge of God did not satisfy the whole person. Though the mind was filled, the heart and emotions were empty.

Many Greeks in John's day had turned to mystery religions, finding emotional stimuli through the senses. By use of lighting, music, incense, and liturgy, various ceremonies promised an emotional union with God. However, it didn't last long. Emotion is a poor foundation; it is too transient. Raw emotion did not satisfy the mind. The worshiper had a great emotional experience over the weekend, but it didn't mean much on Monday morning. If Greeks wanted to know God, they had to choose between a cold rationalism or a passing emotional experience.[35]

John, the last survivor of the 12 apostles, wrote his sermon to emphasize that we can know that we know God. Neither by intellectual theory nor by feeling do we know Him. John believes in visible Christianity—the relationship with God that works out in real life. A popular slogan says, "What you see is what you get!" John, describing the reality of our Christian faith, says, "What you see is what you've got." Real Christianity satisfies because it brings about profound changes in conduct. It consistently builds character. So, "what you see is what you've got." What evidences of knowing God do we look for?

I. THE EVIDENCE OF KNOWING GOD IS TO OBEY HIM

"We know that we have come to know him if we obey his commands. The man who says, 'I know him,' but does not do what he commands is a liar, and the truth is not in him" (vv. 3-4).

John begins with the ring of certainty: "We know." He uses that important word 25 times in his sermon with the meaning, "we perceive." Fifteen more times John says, "We know as a fact." He believed that knowledge of God is not discovered by debate, but by personal relationship with Jesus. "We know that we have come to know him"— John uses the Greek perfect tense suggesting, "We have come to know God, and we still know Him." He refers to a stable relationship with God, a continued "knowing" Him.

John says that knowledge is learned by obedience. Our obedience springs from building on God's Word. The Psalmist sang, "I have hidden your word in my heart that I might not sin against you. . . . Before I was afflicted I went astray, but now I obey your word" (119:11, 67). We need to learn God's Word in order to keep it. We must develop the habit of obedience: "Hereby we do know that we know him, if we keep his commandments" (v. 3, KJV). The Greek grammar implies "if we keep on keeping His commandments." That's a way of life!

The eye is the organ of sight. The ear is the organ of sound reception. But how do we know God? Obedience is the organ of knowing God. Without obedience we do not get to know Him. Dr. L. Nelson Bell, missionary to China, once said, "We may shout from the housetops our faith and orthodoxy, but unless they are coupled with obedience to the teachings of God's Word, there will come a time when we find ourselves rejected from His eternal presence."

During worship services in John's later years, Gnostics would jump up and exclaim, "I know God!"

But John nails them: "What you see is what you've got!" He wrote, "The one who keeps on saying, 'I have come to know Him,' but keeps on not keeping His commandments is a liar." John insists that valid religious experience produces moral changes. When a man's claim contradicts his conduct, he is a liar.

Who learns and learns and acts not what he knows,
Is one who plows and plows but never sows.

"Someone may say, 'I am a Christian; I am on my way to heaven; I belong to Christ.' But if he doesn't do what Christ tells him to, he is a liar" (v. 4, TLB).

A "Dear Abby" column contained a letter from an 11-year-old boy. While his father was away, a playmate claimed he knew how to drive the car in the garage. The boys got the keys and began backing the car out. Just then the mother returned in her little car. The neighbor boy panicked and smashed the big car into the little one.

The son was grounded, punished, and forced to pay for damages. He wrote to "Dear Abby" asking how to regain his parents' trust. Abigail Van Buren gave a classic reply:

"Dear Adam: Start to build your mother's confidence in you by being 100% truthful and responsible. Repeated good behavior will establish you as a trustworthy person. *Words mean nothing. Performance means everything.*"

Obedience is the evidence of knowing God.

II. THE EVIDENCE OF OBEYING GOD IS TO LOVE HIM

"But if anyone obeys his word, God's love is truly made complete in him" (v. 5).

At the Last Supper, Jesus said to His disciples, "Whoever has my commands and obeys them, he is the one who loves me" (John 14:21). Love and obedience cannot be separated.

Biblical love is not a feeling. It's an attitude of obedience and a readiness for action. Don't wait for some "feeling" to motivate you, but begin obeying God. One fellow testified, "I don't know that I have the feeling, but I do have a great desire to obey the Lord, and therefore I must love Him."[36]

As we learn to obey, God perfects His love in us. All of God's commands were given because He loves us. That's why our obedient love is the only adequate response. God's work of perfecting His love in us is a continuing ministry of the Holy Spirit.

John the apostle wasn't always loving. Jesus gave James and John the nickname "Sons of Thunder" (Mark 3:17). The Gospel accounts show them at times as selfish and self-seeking. One time they were so hot-tempered, they wanted to call fire down on a village (Luke 9:54). Even after John moved to Ephesus from Israel, he ran into Cerinthus at the public baths. According to Polycarp, a disciple of John, the apostle cried out, "Let us flee, lest the building fall, since Cerinthus the foe of truth is in it!"[37]

It took John a long time to mature enough to be the

channel of the Holy Spirit for the Gospel and Epistles of love. God worked at perfecting His love in John as he learned obedience.

John adds, "Dear friends, I am not writing you a new command but an old one, which you have had since the beginning. This old command is the message you have heard" (v. 7).

Jesus once said that the greatest commandment was found in Deut. 6:5—"Love the Lord your God with all your heart and with all your soul and with all your strength." And the second most important was found in Lev. 19:18, according to Jesus: "Love your neighbor as yourself." The commandment to love wasn't new. It went back to the beginnings of God's revelation. But old things have a way of fossilizing—commandments became formal and worshipers became duty-bound. Slavish obedience without heart took the place of spontaneous love. Obedience can never substitute for love—only express it.

John continues, "Yet I am writing you a new command; its truth is seen in him and you" (v. 8). The Greeks had two words for "new." One meant "new in time," chronologically new. The other meant "new in quality." The first word might describe the latest car built. But if you bought a car radically different, you would use the second word—new in quality. John was saying, "I am writing you a command new in quality—a radically different kind of love." How is this message of love new in quality?

First, the commandment has a new *emphasis*. In the Old Testament, God's command for His people to love one another was only one of many commandments. Now, in Jesus, this commandment is lifted up and given preeminence. It becomes the summary of all the commandments and their motivation. Love becomes the fulfillment of God's law. Paul calls it the royal law.

Second, the commandment has a new *example.* "Its truth is seen in him and you." Jesus is our Supreme Example, the embodiment of God's command to love. Watch how Jesus loves whenever you need an example on "how to love." Never pick out someone else to compare our love with—we have a tendency to pick someone whose example of love is more of an excuse than a example. Let Jesus be our Model.

There's a tremendous truth in John's statement of love: "Its truth is seen in him and you." God never asks us to do what He would not do. There's no double standard —one for God and one for us. Our conduct should be Christlike, for He works on the same principles He requires of us.

Obedience is tough if someone issues an order and stands back to watch us do all the hard work. When the leader is ready and willing to carry out his own orders, we follow him more readily.

God doesn't sit resting on fluffy pillows in His shrouded heaven, ordering us to love people He wouldn't love. In Jesus, God came to our world, lived in obedience and love, and faced our kind of experiences. Jesus is our great Example in loving.

Third, the commandment has a new *experience.* John's thoughts must have gone back to that Last Supper table with Jesus, when He said, "A new command I give you: Love one another. As I have loved you, so you must love one another. By this all men will know that you are my disciples, if you love one another" (John 13:34-35). Our obedience to God is proved by our love for our brothers. Love must become personified in us. Loving as Jesus did is practical, not primarily emotional. Jesus loved selflessly.

Fourth, the commandment has a new *extent.* Until Jesus came, love was only an obligation to a limited circle of friends and family—or, at the most, one's countrymen. Jesus extended our circle of loving to include everyone. He loved beyond all human barriers and boundary lines. At the Cross we see the height and depth of God's love. In His death and resurrection is the genuineness of His love for all.

To love God is to obey Him. A few years ago the "new morality" was a religious fad. A group of theologians were discussing the idea of being free from any rules and regulations. Some felt the need for some guidelines, and others favored total liberty. During the discussion, they seemed to agree that love was the only acceptable guideline for human conduct. While all these talks went on, a Roman Catholic priest had remained very quiet. One of the fellows turned to him and asked, "Don't you think love is the only limitation on ethical conduct?"

The priest replied in the words of Jesus, "If you love me, you will obey what I command" (John 14:15).

III. THE EVIDENCE OF LOVING GOD IS TO FOLLOW HIM

"This is how we know we are in him: Whoever claims to live in him must walk as Jesus did" (vv. 5-6). I had some difficulty choosing the right word to express John's thought: "must walk as Jesus did." There's a sense in which we must imitate Jesus. However, in the books on words in my library, "to imitate" seems to suggest an artificiality, simply an outward mimicry of Jesus. That is not what John is saying. He is talking about inward conformity. Since the word "walking" refers to total conduct, we are to be Jesus' disciples, His followers, His reproductions. If we really love God, we will follow Jesus Christ, making it a practice to live as He would in our situations.

A word of caution belongs here: no one *becomes* a

Christian by following Jesus' example. We only become Christian by trusting in Him as our Savior and Lord. After we enter His family, we then look to Jesus as our Supreme Example.

The evidence that we are "in Him" is the fact that we are following Him. We are to keep on walking in Him—a continuous way of life, not a spasmodic spurt. Arthur John Gossip said, "If you are not to drift into unconscious hypocrisy, or at least into using great words with little meaning . . . live close to Jesus Christ!" "Whoever claims, 'I am always in union with Him,' ought to live as He lived" (v. 6, Williams).

John adds, "Anyone who claims to be in the light but hates his brother is still in the darkness. . . . But whoever hates his brother is in the darkness and walks around in the darkness; he does not know where he is going, because the darkness has blinded him" (vv. 9, 11).

For the fifth time John speaks of the clash between profession and conduct. Claiming to know God while hating a brother is a living lie; it is not living in the light of God's fellowship. A dairyman described such a person: "He preaches cream but lives skimmed milk." Spurgeon concluded, "An unchanged life is the sign of an uncleansed heart."

Ray Stedman commented:

> If the thief has not stopped his stealing, if the liar has not quit lying, if the alcoholic has not stopped drinking, it is useless for him to claim that he is a Christian. If there has been no basic change in his life, there is nothing that indicates, to him or to anyone else, that he has been delivered from the bondage of Satan and the power of evil into the kingdom of God . . . You can stop these things without being born again, but you cannot be born again without stopping them.[38]

Jesus said, "Not everyone who says to me, 'Lord, Lord,' will enter the kingdom of heaven, but only he who does the will of my Father who is in heaven" (Matt. 7:21).

If we hate our brother, we are refusing to walk with Jesus in the light of God's fellowship. After two neighbors quarreled, one of them built a spite wall 20 feet high to blot out his view of the neighbor. But when the wall was finished, it not only shut out his neighbor, but also shut out the sunlight. Hatred shuts out the sunlight of God's presence in our lives. If one "hates his brother [he] is still in the darkness."

Jesus taught, "But if you do not forgive men their sins, your Father will not forgive your sins" (Matt. 6:15). Resentment turns out the lights. "The darkness has blinded him."

John says of following Jesus: "Whoever loves his brother lives in the light, and there is nothing in him to make him stumble" (v. 10). By honesty with God, living in the light of His fellowship, and following Jesus, we don't become stumbling blocks to ourselves. Harboring resentment, we push ourselves into darkness. Hatred and resentment are self-destructive—and don't make the other fellow feel very good either!

Learning to love as Jesus does, we cease to be a hindrance or stumbling block to others. This kind of love would never put traps or obstacles in the paths of others. There would be no holding back of forgiveness and compassion.

A blind man was seen walking down a dark street, his white cane in one hand tapping the pavement, and a bright flashlight in the other hand. Someone asked him why he carried a flashlight, since he was blind. He replied, "I can't help being blind, but I can help being a stumbling block."[39]

The presence of love in the Christian fellowship was its greatest commendation to those outside. The absence of love is its greatest cause of stumbling. Ray Stedman makes an important point:

> When Christianity has been rejected by the world it is on the basis of a caricature which has been mistaken for the real thing. . . .
>
> The caricature says that the goal of the Christian faith is to produce a heaven filled with stodgy, hymn-singing saints. But the real thing says the goals of Christian faith is to produce love-filled homes right now, filled with strong, manly men and gracious, sweet-tempered women, and orderly, alert, admirable children, who live together facing the normal, useful problems of life with thoughtfulness and mutual dependence upon the activity of a living God in their midst. That is real Christianity.[40]

The goal of knowing God is to love as God loves.

Many Chinese soldiers were severely wounded during the Sino-Japanese War in 1938. Among them was a soldier suffering from a severe gunshot wound of the right knee. When they brought him to the Christian mission hospital, the knee joint was partially exposed to view, badly infected, and in a terrible condition. His military unit was contacted for blood donors so that amputation and transfusion could be done to save his life. No one from his unit would donate to a mere private. It seemed he had little chance to survive.

Meanwhile the chaplain of the Christian mission tried to tell him about the love of the Lord Jesus—but the soldier spurned his concern. Finally a Christian nurse volunteered to give his blood if it were compatible. It was. The soldier received the transfusion, and the operation was a success.

The Chinese soldier was deeply moved that the Christian would give blood to a private when his own people would not do it. When the chaplain came around the next time and talked about Jesus, the soldier gave his heart to the Lord. That act of love by the male nurse was incontrovertible evidence of the truth of the gospel. The soldier had seen the love of Jesus Christ in that medical missionary.

"This is how we know we are in him: Whoever claims to live in him must walk as Jesus did."

To know God is to obey Him.

To obey God is to love Him.

To love God is to follow Him.

6

A Word to the Wise

▽

1 JOHN 2:12-17

△

JOHN'S COMMAND TO love is followed by his re-
minder that love needs boundaries: "Do not love the world
or anything in the world" (v. 15). Why did John say that?
Because "the Christian is not ruined by living in the world,
but by the world living in him." As Lloyd Ogilvie says,
"One of the most difficult challenges for a Christian is to
live in the world without the world living in him."[41] John
speaks a word of warning. Though God's people learn to
love, some things must be hated.

Jesus himself had warned His followers of a basic in-
compatibility: "No one can serve two masters. Either he
will hate the one and love the other, or he will be devoted
to the one and despise the other. You cannot serve both
God and Money" (Matt. 6:24). So John warns us that while
we love God, detrimental things we must not love. A word
to the wise is sufficient!

I. JOHN WARNS US OF WHAT THE WORLD IS

"Do not love the world or anything in the world" (v.
15). That's a shocking statement. Didn't God create this
world and see that "it was very good" (Gen. 1:31)? Didn't
God so love "the world, that he gave his only begotten
Son" (John 3:16, KJV)?

John uses "world" 22 times in this written sermon—and 6 times in this segment. John does not suggest we're to hate the beautiful, intricate, physical world created and kept by God with such loving care. Nor does John suggest hating the world in the sense of the human race with all its need. After all, reaching the world with Jesus is our mission. The Greek word for "world" is *kosmos*, the opposite of the Greek and English word *chaos*. The physical world was chaos until God brought it into order. John refers to "world" in the sense of system, a worldly order. We talk about the "world of sports" or the "world of politics."

The "world" Christians are to hate is that whole system of values and attitudes in rebellion to God that refuses to give Him His rightful place in the hearts of people. Later, John says, "We know that we are children of God, and that the whole world is under the control of the evil one" (1 John 5:19).

In the Upper Room during the Last Supper, Jesus told His disciples, "If the world hates you, keep in mind that it hated me first. If you belonged to the world, it would love you as its own. As it is, you do not belong to the world, but I have chosen you out of the world. That is why the world hates you" (John 15:18-19). The world will never be the natural habitat of the believer.

I enjoy snorkeling and scuba diving. The world under the sea is fascinating and beautiful to me—but I don't belong to that world. I would not make it very long without a nourishing breath of fresh air.

The Christian, though in the world, is not at home there. If it weren't for the Holy Spirit as the Breath of God, we would not survive in this alien world. Without the nourishing of His Word and the lifeline of prayer, we couldn't make it!

Worldliness is that spirit of antagonism to God's com-

mands and laws governing life. Actions or visible characteristics of worldliness are merely symptoms of a rebellious nature. Suppression of conduct, regulations, prohibitions, and taboos may eliminate expressions of rebellion,
but none of them quell the inner defiance.

Here is one of the most abused verses in the Bible: "Do
not love the world or anything in the world." It has been
"used to denounce everything from buttons to beer, from
opera to operations, from the waltz to the watusi."[42]
There's nothing spiritual about wearing clothes 25 years
out-of-date or neglecting one's personal appearance or
flaunting any peculiarities or eccentricities. Much nonsense
has been stereotyped, promoted, and mimicked—all in the
name of holy living. Unless the heart is cleansed and transformed by the grace of God, such behavior is only another
coat of paint on the termite-ridden barn.

The spirit of this world does not look beyond this life.
It looks only for the honors that come from men and is un-
concerned about the honor that comes from God (John
5:44, KJV). This worldly "philosophy . . . is bounded at one
end by a cradle and at the other by a casket. It is centered
only in this life and this world [and this moment]. Jesus
challenged that concept wherever He went and whenever
He spoke. [This philosophy nailed Jesus to the Cross.] According to this philosophy . . . the only important thing is
this life—think how widespread it is today."[43] "Stop loving
this evil world and all that it offers you" (TLB).

II. JOHN WARNS US OF WHAT THE WORLD DOES TO US

"If anyone loves the world, the love of the Father is
not in him. For everything in the world . . . comes not from
the Father but from the world" (vv. 15-16).

First, worldliness begins with an *attitude* of compromise: I try to serve God without offending the devil's crowd! James said, "Don't you know that friendship with the world is hatred toward God? Anyone who chooses to be a friend of the world becomes an enemy of God" (4:4). The world we are not to love is God's rival. We can't keep His smile on our lives while being drawn into the world's spiritual downdraft.

To his beloved church in Ephesus, John wrote the revelation given by Jesus: "Yet I hold this against you: You have forsaken your first love" (Rev. 2:4).

Second, worldliness becomes a matter of our *affections.* Why did John say, "Do not love the world"? Whatever we love affects and shapes our character. Our affections guide our choices.

Choices shape character. John Wesley said, "Whatever cools my affection toward Christ is from the world."

John sounds the danger signal. We say we believe in Jesus and that we love Him, but we turn right around and displace Him in our affections with unsatisfying substitutes. Anything that turns our affection away from the Lord and hinders our spiritual growth expresses our love for the world.

Christians can become vulnerable. In great sorrow, Paul wrote the revealing words: "Demas, in love with this present world, has deserted me" (2 Tim. 4:10, RSV). Even companionship with the apostle Paul did not offset Demas' growing affection for the world. When our affections are placed on the world, we dull our responses to God's love. We then find it difficult to obey His will. Anything—even a good thing—that interrupts fellowship with God must be confessed as sin and surrendered to God.

Third, worldliness tries to gain *attention* by three avenues: "the lust of the flesh, and the lust of the eyes, and the pride of life" (KJV). Satan appeals to our appetites, our imagination, and our vanity.

These natural appetites made their appeal to Jesus Christ, the One without sin. He had not eaten for 40 days. His imagination had been tested with the spectacular. He was tempted to become the greatest by going around the Cross. Friends, don't think we are exempt from temptation.

Worldliness is evidenced by "the lust of the flesh." God made us with natural desires. However, seeking to satisfy desires unnaturally or in conflict with God's moral law shows the world is pulling our affections away from Him. When I decide "that would feel good to me" in spite of its effect on others or on Christ's image in me, I betray my first love for God. While desires are not wrong, "the cravings of sinful man" urge me to go beyond God's moral boundaries, to add something extra, to be dominated by my wants. It's the old attitude that only this life and this moment count.

The Bible says, "His divine power has given us everything we need for life and godliness through our knowledge of him who called us by his own glory and goodness. Through these he has given us his very great and precious promises, so that through them you may participate in the divine nature and escape the corruption in the world caused by evil desires" (2 Pet. 1:3-4).

Worldliness is evidenced by "the lust of the eyes." After a great victory at Jericho, Israel lost an easy battle at the village of Ai. It turned out that one man, Achan, had disobeyed God's command during the battle of Jericho. Achan explained, "When I saw in the plunder a beautiful robe from Babylonia, two hundred shekels of silver and a wedge of gold weighing fifty shekels, I coveted them and took them" (Josh. 7:21). "When I *saw* . . . I *coveted* . . . and [I] *took.*" The lust of the eyes led him into disobedience—and his disobedience led to defeat.

The eyes are a gateway into the mind. When I want something because it looks good to me, my imagination and mind are being tested. Something that looks good or feels good may not *be* good. The desires of the imagination tend to be captivated by outward show. Lavish outward display is no guarantee of reality or happiness.

I served on a District Advisory Board several years ago. At one meeting we were in the process of moving a pastor who had not succeeded in his assignment. But the shocker to me was the comment by a respected business-man: "I just don't understand it. He is such a good dresser. He looks so sharp!"

How's that for real depth? That's how the world in re-bellion to God looks to life. "Don't let the world around you squeeze you into its own mould, but let God re-make you so that your whole attitude of mind is changed" (Rom. 12:2, Phillips).

Worldliness is evidenced by "the pride of life." That's the inner desire that says, "If only I had that, I would really be something!" But Jesus himself warned, "A man's life does not consist in the abundance of his possessions" (Luke 12:15). Life is more than trimmings. Security does not come by "'keeping up with the Joneses,' the desire to have things we do not need, bought with money we do not have, in order to impress people we do not like!"[44]

"The pride of life" creates envy, tempting one to ele-vate himself above others. A false sense of greatness leads one to seek acclaim he does not deserve by character. The more we seek to elevate self, the more energy and interest and money it takes, until our affections end up with our in-vestments: "For where your treasure is, there your heart will be also" (Matt. 6:21). That's a dangerous condition: "If anyone loves the world, the love of the Father is not in him."

Having lost sight of God's love, we cease to love that unique person God created and redeemed us to be. Worldliness creeps up on a believer gradually. First, he becomes a friend of the world. Second, he becomes polluted by the world. Third, he adopts the ways of the world. Fourth, he is in danger of being "condemned with the world" (1 Cor. 11:32).

That's what worldliness does to us.

III. JOHN WARNS US OF WHERE THE WORLD IS GOING

"The world and its desires pass away, but the man who does the will of God lives forever" (v. 17). This old world is a passing parade, a temporary assignment. To place your affections on this world is a foolish choice, because the world of rebellion and godlessness is passing away. The glory of the world is fading fast. How quickly its reins of power pass from one hand to the next. Everything is changing; nothing lasts very long. What a poor investment!

Friends, we had better start learning how to get along without it. We've got eternity ahead of us. That's quite a shock to people living only for the moment!

Genesis 13, 14, and 19 tells the story of Abraham's nephew, Lot. Lot learned the hard way. "First, Lot looked toward Sodom. [Second,] . . . he pitched his tent toward Sodom in the well-watered plains of Jordan. [Third,] . . . he moved into Sodom. And [fourth,] when Sodom was captured by the enemy, Lot was captured too. He was a believer [in God] . . . but he had to suffer with the unbelieving sinners of that wicked city. And when God destroyed Sodom, everything Lot lived for went up in smoke!"[45]

The Bible warns, "Each one should be careful how he builds. . . . his work will be shown for what it is, because the Day will bring it to light. It will be revealed with fire, and the fire will test the quality of each man's work. If what he builds survives, he will receive his reward. If it is burned up, he will suffer loss; he himself will be saved, but only as one escaping through the flames" (1 Cor. 3:10, 13-15).

Putting our love and affection on the things of this old world is a dead-end street. "This world is fading away, and these evil, forbidden things will go with it, but whoever keeps doing the will of God will live forever" (TLB). That doesn't mean that "God's servants will be remembered by future generations. Of the multitudes of famous men who have lived on earth, less than 2,000 have been remembered by any number of people for more than a century."[46] "But he who does the will of God abides for ever" (RSV).

Martin Luther said, "I have held many things in my hands, and I have lost them all. But the things I have placed in God's hands I still possess!" Missionary Jim Elliot, martyred by Auca Indians, wrote: "He is no fool who gives what he cannot keep to gain what he cannot lose."

Jesus reminds us, "But seek first his kingdom and his righteousness, and all these things will be given to you as well" (Matt. 6:33). Paul urges, "Set your affection on things above, not on things on the earth" (Col. 3:2, KJV).

One man confessed, "I have either too much religion or too little. I must either give up what I have or get more. I have too much religion to let me enjoy a worldly life, and too much worldliness to let me enjoy religion." He solved his dilemma by surrendering all to the Lordship of Jesus Christ.

John warns the wise, "Do not love the world . . . The world and its desires pass away, but the man who does the will of God lives forever." You can't help being in the world, but total surrender to Jesus can keep the world out of you!

7

Betrayed with a Kiss

▽

1 JOHN 2:18-27

△

*T*HE BIBLE'S CENTRAL Person from beginning to end is Jesus Christ. As Dr. W. Graham Scroggie said: "Behind the Book was a Person. In the Old Testament He was *predicted;* in the Gospels He was *present;* in the Acts He was *proclaimed;* in the Epistles He was *possessed;* and in the [Revelation] He is *predominant.*"

However, when Jesus walked among men of Israel, one of His close associates forsook Him. Judas walked away from Jesus—and his going gave evidence that he didn't belong with Jesus anymore. In a show of intimacy, Judas betrayed Jesus with a kiss. He got so close but was so far away.

What sustained Jesus in the furnace of opposition? He lived saturated in the Word of God, the Spirit of God, and the fellowship of God.

Decades later, the apostle John sees that the Body of Christ, His Church, is being betrayed. The Church had survived persecution and attacks by the world, but in John's day the Church was being betrayed with a kiss. Nothing can be so insidious as a show of affection from a rebellious heart.

John writes, "Dear children, this is the last hour" (v. 18). We are now about 1,900 years into the "last hour." Jesus referred to two ages—"this present age . . . and . . . the age to come" (Mark 10:30). The present age reaches to the second coming of Jesus. New Testament writers speak of the latter portion of "this present age" as the "last hour," "last days," and "last times."

We must not measure God's time by our clocks and calendars: "With the Lord a day is like a thousand years, and a thousand years are like a day. The Lord is not slow in keeping his promise, as some understand slowness" (2 Pet. 3:8-9). We live in an era of crises, and the Bible simply tells us to be ready for the coming of the Lord anytime. Jesus had warned that His coming would be preceded by an era of tribulation, political upheavals, and social disintegration, a time of apostasy or falling away through the deceptiveness of sin.

Just as an intimate betrayed Jesus in that day, intimates betray Jesus in our day. After urging believers to walk in the light and to talk in love, John insists that genuine Christians must walk in truth. Martin Luther said, "In His life, Christ is an example showing us how to live; in His death, He is a sacrifice satisfying for our sins; in His resurrection, a conqueror; in His ascension, a king; in His intercession, a high priest." These truths unite believers.

Believers may disagree on forms of government, modes of baptism, cultural expressions of worship, etc., but real Christians agree on basic doctrines. Having made an idol out of tolerance, people say, "I'm not interested in doctrine!" How can you walk in truth if you don't know what it is? Your actions spring from your beliefs. If you knew more of God's truth, you might quit breaking your lives and breaking God's heart by wrong living!

Jesus seems destined to be betrayed with a kiss. Let's see what burns in John's heart. The apostle warns believers against spiritual seduction: "Dear children, this is the last hour; and as you have heard that the antichrist is coming, even now many antichrists have come" (v. 18).

John introduces a new word: "antichrist." He is the only New Testament writer to use the word, and he uses it only in his letters. He writes to correct the growing doctrinal error that denied the historic Jesus as God's Son.

The word "Christ" *(christos)* is the same as the Hebrew word "Messiah," meaning "Anointed One." *Antichristos* adds the prefix *anti*, which carries two basic meanings. First, *anti* could mean "against," "over against," or "in opposition to." It suggests an overt opposition against Jesus Christ. The second meaning of *anti* carries the idea "instead of," "in place of," or "substituting for." It suggests a covert or subtle displacement of Jesus Christ. Let's look at both forms of betrayal.

I. OVERT ANTICHRISTS OPPOSE JESUS CHRIST

"As you have heard that the antichrist is coming, even now many antichrists have come. This is how we know it is the last hour. They went out from us, but they did not really belong to us. For if they had belonged to us, they would have remained with us; but their going showed that none of them belonged to us" (vv. 18-19). Overt opposition to Jesus has several characteristics.

First, errors openly opposing Christ *began within the Christian circle*. Most of today's false cults and anti-Christian movements have begun with their founders in a church circle. "They went out from us" and started their own groups. Islam and Communism both took root in a sterile, lifeless church. Ardent anti-Christian spokesman Nikita Khrushchev once wrote a thesis on John 15. You'd be surprised at the background of many people bent on opposing Jesus Christ.

Second, errors openly opposing Christ *seem to appear in cycles* during the course of church history. However, the cycles are getting closer and closer together. The frequency of error is on the increase.

Third, errors openly opposing Christ *use Christian terminology to seduce believers away from Jesus Christ.* Beginning in Christian circles, they pick up the language but substitute other meanings.

Cerinthus, contemporary of John and spokesman for the Gnostic heresy that John combated, talked about believing in Jesus Christ. But Cerinthus meant that the divine Christ came upon the human Jesus at baptism and departed before Jesus' death. To the Gnostics, the man Jesus and the divine Christ were two separate persons—but their use of the word sounded right at first.

A classic example is the founder of Christian Science, Mary Baker Eddy. "Though she uses perfectly normal Christian words she invests them with an entirely different meaning, and in order to explain that meaning she . . . publish[ed] a glossary of terms at the end of her book. Words . . . in the dictionary . . . universally taken to mean one thing are, in her book, given a specialized meaning . . . [departing] from essential Christian doctrine. This is common practice in many cults today."[47]

"Cultists tend to take certain peripheral truths . . . and . . . elevate them to a prominence far greater than they deserve, whereas matters of major importance are played down."[48]

Fourth, errors openly opposing Christ *make an abrupt break with historic Christianity and its basic beliefs.* Of course, the cultists insist they are the enlightened ones, the mainstream of godliness, but they sever fellowship and voluntarily break the outward bonds. "For if they had belonged to us, they would have remained with us; but their going showed that none of them belonged to us" (v. 19). Suspect any group that breaks away from a Bible-believing church to follow human leaders and extrabiblical books and writings.

Dr. Harry Ironside noted, "Many . . . advocates of these unholy systems were once numbered among the Christian company. They took their places at the communion table, had fellowship outwardly with the people of God, went through Christian baptism, but now have turned away from [biblical] Christianity . . . from the simplicity . . . in Christ, and [denied] the precious blood that once they confessed."[49]

The author of Hebrews has these awesome words: "It is impossible for those who have once been enlightened, who have tasted the heavenly gift, who have shared in the Holy Spirit, who have tasted the goodness of the word of God and the powers of the coming age, if they fall away, to be brought back to repentance, because to their loss they are crucifying the Son of God all over again and subjecting him to public disgrace" (6:4-6). Even yet Jesus is betrayed with a kiss!

John was not writing about nameless foes but about people whom John and his readers had known and loved in the Body of Christ. The kiss of betrayal brought deep pain and brokenness to the Christians. Nothing hurts quite like the loss of fellowship in Christ!

Fifth, errors openly opposing Christ, in one form or another, *deny Christ's authority.* He is not the heretics' ultimate authority. They seek sources to shed light on God's Word—dreams, visions, and secret revelations usurp the authority of Christ. Jesus is devalued while other mediators between God and man are brought to the fore.

Sixth, errors openly opposing Christ *boldly attempt to seduce genuine Christians.* One writer noted, "Antichristian groups rarely try to lead lost sinners to their false faith. Instead, they spend much of their time trying to convert professing Christians to their own doctrines. They are out to 'seduce' the faithful . . . We have been warned that this would happen."[50] "But the Holy Spirit tells us clearly that in the last times some in the church will turn away from Christ and become eager followers of teachers with devil-inspired ideas. These teachers will tell lies with straight faces and do it so often that their consciences won't even bother them" (1 Tim. 4:1-2, TLB).

These are some of the characteristics of those who openly oppose Jesus Christ. However, John warns of a more subtle danger.

II. COVERT ANTICHRISTS SUBSTITUTE OTHER THINGS IN PLACE OF JESUS CHRIST

Those who openly oppose Christ can be openly confronted. One knows where the lines are drawn. But John's greatest concern, his reason for writing this segment, is the person who in subtle, quiet, inward ways puts something in place of Jesus. Having a substitute loyalty, he may yet be in the church but not be of the real Spirit of Christ.

"Who is the liar? It is the man who denies that Jesus is the Christ. Such a man is the antichrist—he denies the Father and the Son. No one who denies the Son has the Father; whoever acknowledges the Son has the Father also. . . . I am writing these things to you about those who are trying to lead you astray" (vv. 22-23, 26). Covert opposition to Jesus has several characteristics.

First, undercover error *espouses the greatness of man and his potential apart from God.* Given a little time and lucky breaks, man will lift himself out of the miry clay. Man worships his own achievements—and then himself. But what a faulty foundation! Thinking good thoughts is all right, but alone and without God, good thoughts are like whistling in the dark. Good thoughts will never meet the deep spiritual need of mankind. Joshua Liebman, author of the bestseller *Peace of Mind*, committed suicide.

Man's tinkering can't solve the problem of a God-created soul. It has been noted that man

> can build an automobile, complete in its technological perfection, but if he puts a driver in the seat who cannot handle it, within moments that beautiful automobile is a mass of wreckage. With the automobile we are killing thousands of people a year, but instead of solving the problem with the driver we are trying to solve it by improving the car.
>
> Right here is where philosophies and pseudo-Christian heresies come in. Every philosophy, every cult, and every heresy . . . attempt[s] to reveal how man can achieve greatness, how he can fulfill himself . . . Each of them launches upon what they call "a search for truth." They are looking for the key to all things. They are examining the mystery of existence . . . to discover the secrets of the universe, looking for that which can give purpose and meaning to life. Lacking the necessary equipment and refusing to acknowledge the need for another teacher beyond man, superior to man, they became those whom Paul describes as "ever learning, and never able to come to the knowledge of the truth" (2 Tim. 3:7, KJV).[51]

That's humanism—man's attempt to fill the emptiness of the heart. It doesn't work. To the question, "Are you a Christian?" the humanist replied, "I am trying to be a Christian." Trying is the opposite of trusting. Trusting is the way of grace—the way of Christ. Trying is the way of achievement.

Second, undercover error *likes Jesus but denies His deity*. "Who is the liar? It is the man who denies that Jesus is the Christ. Such a man is the antichrist—he denies the Father and the Son" (v. 22). Reducing Jesus to mere status of a good man destroys the reality of Christ. To rank Jesus alongside Buddha, Muhammad, and Confucius, or to deny the Atonement for our sins in Jesus' death on the Cross, makes a mockery of God's Word. Sadly, many people teach about Jesus, give lessons on love, attempt to follow His ethical precepts, have their names on church membership rolls, and can do the ceremonies by rote—but still have not accepted Jesus as Savior and Lord. That's putting something in place of Christ.

Some people say, "We worship God, but we don't accept Jesus as God's Son." John says, "Such a man is the antichrist—he denies the Father and the Son. No one who denies the Son has the Father" (vv. 22-23). Jesus himself had taught: "I and the Father are one" (John 10:30). Earlier, Jesus said, "He who does not honor the Son does not honor the Father, who sent him" (John 5:23). You can't have One without the Other! Only as we understand Jesus do we understand the character of the Father. If we reject Jesus' revelation of the Father, we are left with "an oblong blur" for a God.

If Jesus isn't God in human flesh, His death has no meaning. We are left with an empty shell. Someone wrote, "If Christ is not true God equally with the Father, there is no essential difference between Christianity and pagan polytheism." Antichrists deny Jesus' deity in order to make Him acceptable to an ungodly world.

Third, undercover error *undermines faith in Jesus with a divisive or critical attitude.* Habitually critical people are destructive to the household of faith. A critical spirit is anti-Christian—but apparently socially acceptable. Its infection spreads like a virus from person to person. Negative attitudes express a lack of trust in Christ's power. But, friends, this is still the age of miracles. As one said, "Christ can change difficult people and transform troublesome problems."[52] Jesus is ready and able. Whatever Christ did, He is able to do today.

Fourth, undercover error *substitutes self-justification in place of Jesus' cross*. When Jesus announced His coming death on the Cross, Peter rebuked Jesus: "Never, Lord! . . . This shall never happen to you!" (Matt. 16:22).

Though He did not welcome a shameful death, Jesus responded: "Get behind me, Satan! You are a stumbling block to me; you do not have in mind the things of God, but the things of men" (v. 23).

The anti-Christian avoids confronting the cross of Christ. He doesn't wish to admit his spiritual poverty.

> Faith is no longer considered as the free gift of God to the unworthy sinner, but a reward which has been earned by the faithful keeping of various conditions and requirements. [Elaborate methods of self-justification begin.] We rationalize our sins and deny our need for the cross. [The anti-Christian says,] in reality, we are our own saviors. God ought to accept us for our goodness, productivity, and faithfulness. Good Friday is a troublesome day [to the anti-Christian. He thinks] if we had been the only people alive in Jerusalem that day, [surely] it would not have been necessary.[53]

And, anti-Christians "live and work as if [they] can make it on [their] own. Prayer is spasmodic. [Their] security is drawn from [their] positions, popularity, or possessions. Most telling of all is [their] dumbness about [their] faith in daily conversation. How could anyone know what [they] believe? [They] communicate the impression that what [they] have and are is the result of talent and hard work."[54]

If common sense had been enough to save us, Jesus would not have gone to the Cross.

Fifth, undercover error *attempts to take Christ's place by making people dependent upon us rather than on Jesus*. Even with good intentions and great compassion, we can help people in a way that makes them dependent upon our presence or decision making or comfort. I've observed, even among good people, overgrown mothering or smothering instincts that were baited hooks. "Our need to be needed prompts us to try to be the answer to people's needs. We insulate people from the reality of their desperate condition."[55]

Pastors, parents, teachers, friends, and neighbors all face the possibility of becoming a substitute for Christ. We must break that unhealthy dependency, even if it means someone else must lead others to Jesus. He is the only safe center for anyone's life. John adds, "I am writing these things to you about those who are trying to lead you astray" (v. 26). Sometimes we unthinkingly lead others astray by allowing them to become too dependent on us instead of Jesus.

Sixth, undercover error *often accepts a cafeteria-type basis for truth*—picking and choosing among the Scriptures those truths we like and rejecting those we dislike. If we're going to walk in God's truth, we must be open to all of His truth. People have a way of riding hobby horses—or playing a song on one string. God's truth is the whole Bible—not just the parts we like best!

Jesus reminded us that we are nourished "on every word that comes from the mouth of God" (Matt. 4:4). Paul said, "All Scripture is God-breathed [inspired by God, RSV, etc.] and is useful for teaching, rebuking, correcting and training in righteousness, so that the man of God may be thoroughly equipped for every good work" (2 Tim. 3:16-17).

God's commandments are still in effect. He hasn't changed or rescinded one of them. Lying; cheating; unholy use of His name; working on the Lord's day; murdering adults, children, or unborn babies are still wrong. All these prohibitions came from the mind of God—and He hasn't changed His mind. He still plans for His people to live in the beauty of holiness, in the image of Christ, and unspotted in this world. Social mores cannot change God's mind. Conclusions of pollsters do not alter one iota of His immutable plan for restoring broken humanity: total dependence upon the atoning death and resurrection of Jesus Christ. If you are going to take God at His Word, you must take His whole Word.

Charles Colson said it straightforwardly in his book *Born Again:*

> Once faced with the staggering proposition that [Jesus] is God, I was cornered, all avenues of retreat blocked, no falling back to that comfortable middle ground about Jesus being a great moral teacher. If He is not God, He is nothing, least of all a great moral teacher. For what He taught includes the assertion that He is indeed God. And if He is not, that one statement alone would have to qualify as the most monstrous lie of all time—stripping Him at once of any possible moral platform.

> I could not . . . take Him on a slightly lower plateau because it is easier to do so, less troublesome to my intellect, less demanding of my faith, less challenging to my life. That would be substituting my mind for His, using Christianity where it helped to buttress my *own* notions, ignoring it where it didn't.

> I realized suddenly that there is less heresy in rejecting Him altogether, dismissing Him as a raving lunatic . . . than to remake Him into something He wasn't [and isn't]. Jesus said take it, all or nothing. If I was to believe in God at all, I had to take Him as He reveals Himself, not as I might wish Him to be.[56]

Have you taken Jesus seriously? Have you taken Him as He has revealed himself or only as He fits comfortably into your own ideas? In Christ, God became Man to give us a concrete, definite idea of what kind of person to think of when we think of God. Christ is the visible expression of the invisible God. Byron the poet touched on Jesus' deity and humanity when he said, "If ever a man were God or God were man, Jesus was both."

The spirit of Antichrist simply puts someone or something or even oneself in God's rightful place. As Jesus stoops to speak to you today, will you betray Him with a kiss of pretended affection or embrace Him as Savior and Lord?

8

Kept by Continuing

▽

1 JOHN 2:18-27

△

*J*OHN R. PRICE gave unfinished parables:

> A man got married. After the honeymoon, he disappeared. His wife heard nothing from him except that she received a check from him once a month. One evening he walked in, kissed her, and sat down to be fed. She was incensed. Bewildered, the man asked, "What's the matter? I married you, didn't I? I told you I love you. I send you a check every month. What more do you want?"
>
> A child enrolled in school. For several days he was absent. When the truant officer came around, his mother said, "Oh, we feel Jimmy can be as good a scholar at home as at school, so we let him play in the backyard and learn from nature."
>
> A man volunteered for the army, took the oath of allegiance, and was inducted. But he failed to report for duty. When the military police came, he said, "I've been shooting guns since I was a kid . . . You just call me when you're ready to fight."
>
> And, once upon a time, a family joined the church . . .[57]

These unfinished parables describe failure and loss. Each situation could have been saved by continuing or remaining.

We enter the Christian life by being born again. We are kept by continuing in Christ. Paul urges, "Just as you received Christ Jesus as Lord, continue to live in him, rooted and built up in him" (Col. 2:6). Saved by grace, we are kept by continuing in His grace.

John introduces another key word: "remain." Sometimes translated "abide" or "continue," the word "remain" expresses a continuing relationship, not simply an encounter or a crisis moment with Jesus. God has given resources by which we may be kept.

I. THE FIRST RESOURCE IS THE ABIDING WORD OF GOD

"All of you know the truth. I do not write to you because you do not know the truth, but because you do know it and because no lie comes from the truth. . . . See that what you have heard from the beginning remains in you" (vv. 20-21, 24).

We are kept by continuing in God's Word. The One dwelling in us knows the truth and applies it to us as we walk with Him. The Christian need not succumb to error, for we have God's Word as an abiding resource.

God teaches us His Word and enables us to intuitively know His truth. John wrote, "And all of you know the truth" (v. 20). Believers do not possess all truth, but they all possess knowledge of spiritual truth. Gnostics had boasted that they alone knew the truth. God gives truth to all His children: Jesus is "the true light that gives light to every man" (John 1:9).

John urges believers to walk in truth. Truth never fears the light of exposure. The more light is turned on to truth, the clearer it becomes. Sunlight on a dead log speeds up the process of decay and decomposition. But sunlight on a living tree stimulates its growth and beauty and life. The more God's Word scouts out our inner person, the more open and honest we are free to become.

John attacked the spirit of "antichrist," but he does not wish to leave believers asking, "Is it I?" John speaks a note of reassurance: "I do not write to you because you do not know the truth, but because you do know it" (v. 21). John has great confidence in the capacity of God's people to comprehend His Word.

God's Word is more than a message heard and accepted in the past. The message must continue to be present and active in the believer's life. Continual study and instruction in the Word are important for continuing in the faith.

"See that what you have heard from the beginning remains in you" (v. 24). For God's Word to remain in you requires more than a mechanical, dutiful reading of so many pages of the Bible. The word "remain" or "abide" means literally "to possess." When a guest comes into our home, we say, "Make yourself at home." In other words, "Possess this house as though it were yours!"

We must allow God's Word to make itself at home in our hearts. God can say anything He wishes. He can do with us anything He desires. Our heart is His dwelling place.

If we are going to accept His words, we must accept them all. There's dynamic power in God's abiding Word.

A liberal English minister had just gone to bed. A knock came to his door. A poor, wretched young girl stood dripping wet from the rain. She asked, "Are you the minister?"

He replied, "Yes."

She asked, "Would you come and get my mother in?"

The pastor said, "I've already gone to bed. If your mother is drunk, call a policeman to get her in."

"You don't understand!" she exclaimed. "My mother is not out in this storm. She isn't drunk. She is at home dying—but she's afraid to die. She's afraid she's lost. My mother wants to go to heaven, but doesn't know how. I told her I'd find a minister to get her in."

He thought to himself, "What a discomfort to go out in the storm! What a risk to be seen with this bedraggled girl in the red-light district." Worried about what his people might think, he said, "Go down to the rescue mission. The superintendent there will help you. He lives in your neighborhood."

The young girl replied, "He may be a good man, but I don't know him. I promised Mother I'd bring a real minister. Come quickly! Mother is dying!"

Unable to resist and feeling ashamed, the pastor agreed to go. At last they got to the slum district, went into an old house, up a rickety stairway, and along a dark hall to a little room.

The dying woman looked up and said, "Oh, sir, can you do anything for a poor old sinner? I've been wicked all my life. I'm going to hell. I want to be saved. I want to go to heaven. What can I do?"

Telling of the incident later, the minister said, "I stood there looking down at the poor anxious face, and thought, 'Whatever will I tell her!' I had been preaching in my own church on salvation by character and good works, by culture and human determination. I can't tell her about salvation by character and good works—she doesn't have any. I can't tell her about salvation by culture—she has no time for that. I can't tell her about salvation by human determination—she's gone too far.

"Then it came to me, 'Why not tell her what my mother used to tell me? She's dying and it can't hurt her—even if it does her no good.' And so I said, 'My poor woman, God is gracious. The Bible says, "God so loved the world, that he gave his only begotten Son, that whosoever believeth in him should not perish, but have everlasting life"' (John 3:16, KJV).

"She said, 'Does the Bible say that? Then this ought to get me in. But, sir, my sins! What about my sins?'

"Amazingly, verses came to me—verses I had learned years ago and never used. I said, 'The blood of Jesus Christ his Son cleanseth us from all sin' (1 John 1:7, KJV).

"She asked, 'All sin? Does it really say that His blood will cleanse me from *all* sin? That ought to get me in!'

"'Christ Jesus came into the world to save sinners; of whom I am chief' (1 Tim. 1:15, KJV).

"'Well,' she said. 'If the chief sinner got in, I can come to Jesus, too. Pray for me!'

"I knelt down and prayed with that poor woman—and *got her in.* While I was getting her in, I got in myself. We two poor sinners, minister and dying harlot, were saved together in that little room."[58]

We have a great resource in God's Word. How wonderful and powerful it is in those who keep His Word remaining in their hearts.

II. THE SECOND RESOURCE IS THE ABIDING SPIRIT OF GOD

"But you have an anointing from the Holy One . . . As for you, the anointing you received from him remains in you, and you do not need anyone to teach you. But as his anointing teaches you about all things and as that anointing is real, not counterfeit—just as it has taught you, remain in him" (vv. 20, 27).

We are kept by continuing in God's anointing. This wonderful anointing of the Spirit sets us apart for God's use. The gift of the Holy Spirit is God's all-sufficient means for helping believers have a knowledge of the truth. The verb "to anoint" is *chriō*. *Chriō* is the root for "Christ," which means "The Anointed One." "Christians" are "anointed ones." We are kept by the Spirit's anointing.

In Old Testament times, a priest or king was inducted into office by being anointed with oil, symbol of God's Spirit. "As for you, the anointing you received from him remains in you" (v. 27). The Holy Spirit *is* our anointing. The Greek grammar to "you received" suggests an *act*, not a *process*. It is an anointing we receive as a gift. We do not earn it. God's abiding Spirit, making himself at home in our hearts, is the answer to Jesus' prayer: "And I will ask the Father, and He will give you another Counselor to be with you forever—the Spirit of truth. . . . you know him, for he lives with you and will be in you" (John 14:16-17).

By yielding to God's control and guidance, we are kept by the abiding presence of the Holy Spirit. His power is made available to us by faith.

Jesus told His disciples, "But the Counselor, the Holy Spirit, whom the Father will send in my name, will teach you all things and will remind you of everything I have said to you" (John 14:26). Though false teachers insisted that only they had the secret to spiritual truth, John says, "The anointing you received from him remains in you, and you do not need anyone to teach you" (v. 27). His Spirit enables us to know and recognize truth.

One day Simon confessed aloud, "You are the Christ, the Son of the living God."

Jesus responded joyfully, "Blessed are you, Simon . . . for this was not revealed to you by man, but by my Father in heaven" (Matt. 16:16-17).

God's Word, in the hands of God's Spirit, has a tremendous capacity to correct error and to guide believers into His truth. The Holy Spirit confirms the truth found in Scripture. He never contradicts Scripture.

A missionary to American Indians came to Los Angeles with an Indian friend, a new Christian. As they walked down the street, they passed a man on the corner preaching with Bible in hand. The missionary knew the man represented a cult, but the Indian saw only the Bible. He stopped to listen to the sermon.

The missionary thought to himself as he began to pray, I hope my friend doesn't get confused. In a few minutes the Indian turned away from the street preacher and joined his missionary friend.

"What did you think of the preacher?" the missionary asked.

"All the time he was talking," exclaimed the Indian, "something in my heart kept saying, 'Liar! Liar!'"

The Holy Spirit guides us into truth and helps us to recognize error. This anointing of God is "no lie," because "the Spirit is the truth" (1 John 5:6).[59]

As Paul Rees put it, "The Holy Spirit enlightens and directs . . . most easily and most surely those who know their Bibles most thoroughly."

III. THE THIRD RESOURCE IS THE ABIDING FELLOWSHIP OF GOD

"See that what you have heard from the beginning remains in you. If it does, you also will remain in the Son and in the Father. And this is what he promised us—even eternal life. . . . remain in him" (vv. 24-25, 27).

We are kept by continuing in fellowship with Jesus Christ. If you remain in Christ, you have eternal life—and you don't need anything more. That continuing fellowship with God guides you into all truth.

In 1808 Alexander, czar of Russia, met with Napoleon in the Palace of Erfurt to seal an imperial alliance. Over the throne was the inscription, "The friendship of a great man is a gift from the gods." Under that banner, Alexander and Napoleon exchanged vows of friendship and loyalty. It turned out to be a hollow mockery. A little later the armies of Alexander and Napoleon marched against each other.

However, friendship with Jesus is no empty show. When we receive Him, He is our Friend for better or for worse, through good times and tough times. You can depend on Him.

John's command, "Remain in him" (v. 27), echoes Jesus' words to His disciples on the eve of His death: "Remain in me, and I will remain in you. No branch can bear fruit by itself; it must remain in the vine. Neither can you bear fruit unless you remain in me. . . . If you remain in me and my words remain in you, ask whatever you wish, and it will be given you. . . . remain in my love" (John 15:4, 7, 9). This is why Christianity is so different from other religions. You can take the founders out of the others, but if we take Jesus out of the Good News, we have nothing. Fellowship with Jesus establishes our faith.

An agnostic professor of comparative religions asked a Christian convert, "What have you found in Christianity that your old religion didn't have?"

Sundar answered, "I have Christ!"

Impatiently, the professor tried again. "Yes, but what principles or doctrines have you found that you didn't have before?"

Sundar replied, "The unique thing I have found is Christ."

World religions have many fine things—but they don't have Christ.[60] We are kept by continuing in Jesus Christ.

Dr. E. Stanley Jones was preaching in one of the Indian states. . . . The Hindu prime minister, as chairman [of the meeting], said in his opening introduction: "I shall reserve my remarks for the close of the address; for no matter what

[Dr. Jones] says, I will find parallel things in our own sacred books. . . ." [However], at the close of the meeting he was [stymied]. Dr. Jones did not present "things"; he presented a Person—Jesus—and that Person [isn't] found in their sacred books.

What is new in Christianity? . . . [Jesus!] That's why [our] gospel is "Good News."[61]

If you remain in Christ, who is the Truth, you can't get by so easily anymore. Ray Stedman noted, "Sooner or later you must explain your actions to Him. . . . All those wonderful excuses that went over so smoothly with your wife or husband or friends or neighbors sound very lame when repeated to [Jesus]. He is totally unimpressed by them. He does not say anything; He simply folds His arms and looks at you . . . When you feel His eyes upon you, all your excuses sound . . . weak."[62]

Living with Jesus opens our lives to His searchlight of truth. As He brings all things to light, we only have two alternatives—confession or denial. In response to our open confession, Jesus brings healing and wholeness.

"If you obey little, you will experience little. If you obey much, you will experience much."[63]

Stedman gives good insight:

Since God gives Himself to us in the same degree as we give ourselves to Him . . . three things result . . . : First, you can have all that [Jesus] is, if you are ready to take Him. . . .

Second, . . . you will have only as much as you are satisfied with. God . . . never give[s] you more than you really want. God never forces blessings upon anyone.

Third, . . . you now have . . . all that you really want from God. Your present level of life is an indication of what you want . . . If your life is not satisfying to you as a Christian, it is not God's fault. . . . You are not yet willing, for one reason or another, to take from Him all He [desires] to give, out of [His] fullness.[64]

To know Him, we must live close to Him. A middle-aged couple rode along in the car. She remembered their romance of earlier days. Eyeing the distance that separated them in the front seat of the car, she said, "When we were first married, we used to sit close in the car."

He replied, "I'm not the one who moved away."

Are you enjoying fellowship with Jesus? If not, remember He's not the one who moved away! We are kept by continuing fellowship with Him.

God has given us great resources for spiritual growth and spiritual conquest: His abiding Word, His abiding Spirit, and His abiding fellowship. "Remain in him."

9

God Isn't Finished
with Me Yet

▽

1 JOHN 2:28—3:3

△

I FIND A SENSE of relief in the bumper sticker, "Be patient—God isn't finished with me yet." I'm glad I'm not what I was, and I'm excited that I'm not yet what I'm going to be through Jesus Christ! My inadequacies and imperfections someday won't seem so glaring in light of what God is going to make of me: "Dear friends, now we are children of God, and what we will be has not yet been made known. But we know that when he appears, we shall be like him" (1 John 3:2). Some of you may wonder why God doesn't hurry up and get started. You are not alone. We all have our moments, but our times are in God's hands.

Some Hindus taunted a Christian convert in an Indian train station: "Why didn't you stay in your own religion and improve it?"

The Christian replied, "I don't want a religion I have to improve. I want a religion that improves me—and I found that in Jesus Christ!"

In spite of aspirations to be like Jesus, our failures remind us that God hasn't finished reshaping our raw materials.

Having described the Christian life as "walking in the

light," the apostle John explained that confession of sin clears up any hindrance in our fellowship with the Lord. When I confessed my need for Christ's forgiveness, I did not reach the heights of my faith. It was only a beginning. God has more up ahead. His work had just begun in my life. And now John throws open the windows on new vistas—reasons for rejoicing!

I. I REJOICE IN GOD'S UNBROKEN FELLOWSHIP

John begins, "And now, dear children" (2:28). That's his way of marking a new section of his written sermon. "And now, dear children, continue in him" (v. 28). Or, paraphrased, "Stay in happy fellowship with the Lord" (TLB). The Christian might sin, but it is good news that he need not sin. I can remain in unbroken, happy fellowship with the Lord.

The word "continue" is important in John's writings. It suggests "to dwell" or "rest in." I continue in unbroken fellowship with God: first, by believing His truth; second, by obeying His truth; and third, by loving His family. If I find myself out of fellowship with Him, it is easy to figure out why. I have either believed a lie, disobeyed His Word, or lacked love for a fellow child of God. The solution is to confess my sin instantly and to accept His immediate forgiveness: "If we confess our sins, he is faithful and just and will forgive us our sins and purify us from all unrighteousness" (1:9).

If we continue in the Lord, "When he appears we may be confident and unashamed before him at his coming" (2:28). John points out two characteristics of our unbroken fellowship with God.

First, in our unbroken fellowship with God we can be

"confident." The Greek word John used for "confident" carries the idea of frankness, freedom to speak honestly and openly with God. We don't have to say one thing to God while we feel another way. In secular Greek this word for "confident" described the kind of boldness and freedom of expression first made possible in the Greek democracy.

The author of Hebrews wrote: "Therefore, brothers, since we have confidence to enter the Most Holy Place by the blood of Jesus, by a new and living way opened for us . . . let us draw near to God with a sincere heart in full assurance of faith" (10:19-20, 22). Also, "Let us then approach the throne of grace with confidence" (4:16). Let's not tread on this wonderful privilege with irreverent or ungrateful feet.

Second, in our unbroken fellowship with God, we can be "unashamed before him at his coming." Literally, John says we need not "shrink from him in shame" (RSV). If we live carelessly, we have reason to be ashamed to face Him. Because of spiritual failure, we may be accepted as a child of God but not acceptable to Him.

I visited in a home where the little boys had disobeyed by getting dirty in careless play just before the Sunday evening service. When they came into the parsonage, they were not acceptable in that condition, but they were accepted as children of that family. The process of getting them cleaned up began *immediately!*

When we come to God and admit our uncleanness, He immediately goes to work to clean us up "and purify us from all unrighteousness" (1:9). John has already written, "My dear children, I write this to you so that you will not sin. But if anybody does sin, we have one who speaks to the Father in our defense—Jesus Christ, the Righteous One" (2:1). Through Him we can continue in unbroken fellowship with God. Paul wrote, "So we make it our goal to please him" (2 Cor. 5:9).

Continuing in God's love and truth, we don't need to be fearful in His presence. Paul wrote to young Timothy, "For God did not give us a spirit of timidity" (2 Tim. 1:7). As God's children, we hold Him in reverence and do not deliberately choose to disobey Him or try His patience.

Warren Wiersbe told of a group of teenagers enjoying a party. Someone suggested going to a certain rowdy restaurant for a good time. Jan said to her date, "I'd rather you took me home. My parents don't approve of that place."

One of the girls asked sarcastically, "Afraid your father will hurt you?"

"No," Jan responded. "I'm not afraid my father will hurt me, but I don't want to hurt him."[65]

She illustrates the principle that a child of God has no desire to sin against His love. In the same way, "we may be confident and unashamed before him." "Stay in happy fellowship with the Lord." We can live at ease in Jesus' presence with no last-minute rush to catch up before He returns to receive His children.

Phillips Brooks said, "The way to prepare to meet God is to live with Him now so that to meet Him later will be nothing strange." We can live in unbroken fellowship with Him.

II. I REJOICE IN GOD'S EXTRAVAGANT LOVE

"How great is the love the Father has lavished on us, that we should be called children of God!" (3:1). God's love for us is so unparalleled that John exclaimed in Greek, literally, "Behold, of what country" or "From what far realm!" "What unearthly love!" God's love is so extravagant that it is beyond explanation; it is foreign to this world's way of thinking and understanding. He extends His love to the unlovely and unworthy. We receive so much at the hand of our Heavenly Father!

Love is more than a noun. Love is an action verb. Love does something for another's welfare. The popular idea of love as an emotion—something you feel inside—is not the biblical idea of love. To realize "how great is the love the Father has lavished on us," think how God has acted in our behalf. The whole Christ-event expresses His love in action.

Why does He do it? "That we should be called children of God!" More than a name tag, "children of God" means that God calls and we respond in obedience. It isn't a label put on us as a finished product—perfect and complete. He isn't finished with us yet—we are but *children of God.*"

Both Paul and John refer to believers as "children of God," but they used two different words. Paul spoke of "children" *(uios)* in a legal sense—emphasizing the idea of adoption into God's family. Here, however, John used another Greek word *(tekna)*, which suggests being a child by birth. John's emphasis is on the "new birth." Christians are products of God's love—they are born of the Spirit.

Some people may wonder, "Isn't every person a child of God?" No! While that makes beautiful sentiment, God never calls all persons His children. The Bible tells us how we become "children of God": "You are all sons [children] of God through faith in Christ Jesus" (Gal. 3:26). Only the one who has exercised faith in Jesus is ever called a child of God. He is not "the Father of all mankind." He is the Creator of all mankind. The Good News is that all may become His children. There's room in His heart for you!

"See how very much our heavenly Father loves us, for

he allows us to be called his children—think of it—and we really *are!*" (3:1, TLB). Athanasius exclaimed, "Jesus became what we are in order that He might make us what He is." During public prayer, one of our men said, "God sent Jesus to be the Son of Man so that we can be sons of God." I don't know where he got that, but it's true!

I rejoice in God's extravagant love. I want to be responsive to His voice in my life. He isn't finished with me yet! I'm learning—and I'm learning to listen.

III. I REJOICE IN GOD'S CONTINUING WORK

John says, "Dear friends, now we are children of God, and what we will be has not yet been made known" (3:2). The emphatic word of that sentence is the word "now." In the Greek text, it is the first word of the sentence. Usually the first word is the word to be emphasized in a Greek sentence. "*Now* we are children of God"! Eternal life belongs to us *now*. We are not waiting until we die to get it. When we are born again, we have Christ's life in us *now*. We are heirs of God's promises and glory *now*—not in some distant future.

Since we are *now* God's children, He is at work on us *now* to make us more like Jesus. If we don't push His hand away and rebel, God is remaking us day by day. Sometimes that process is painful. That's the kind of tough love parents need when Johnny insists on playing in the middle of a busy street. They don't stop loving him because he plays there. Love demands, "Johnny, this isn't the place to play. You'll get hit by a car. So, I'm going to spank you to save you from something far worse."

From the very beginning, God has shown that quality of love. Through His prophets and His Son, He says, "I love you. Nothing can change that. But My standards are righteousness and justice. Unless you meet them, there will be some hard consequences." Sometimes He chastens us because He cares too much to leave us to ourselves. I am glad He isn't finished with me yet!

"And what we will be has not yet been made known." Children must grow and develop. The unknown future stretches out ahead. Who can guess the possibilities? "No eye has seen, no ear has heard, no mind has conceived what God has prepared for those who love him" (1 Cor. 2:9). He has a lot more going for us!

God is at work in our lives like the artist who began to paint his masterpiece. He stretched a canvas across one side of his large studio, put up the scaffolding, and began painting with great sweeps of his brush, putting in the background.

After several days of work, he stood back to view his progress. A visitor stopped in for a moment. The artist asked, "What do you think of that picture? That's going to be the masterpiece of my career. Isn't it magnificent?"

The visitor gawked and replied, "I don't see anything but a lot of big daubs of paint—gray here and blue there. What is it?"

"Oh, I forgot," said the artist. "You can only see what is there, while I can see the picture as it is going to be."

"We are already God's children, right now, and we can't even imagine what it is going to be like later on" (3:2, TLB). A person's conversion is the miracle of a moment; the growth of a saint is the task of a lifetime. One day God's work shall be completed, but for now, we are being changed. Christian, are you discouraged because your spiritual progress seems so slow? Be patient—God isn't finished with you yet! Some day He will bring it all to completion, and the glory of His showroom will be worth all the time spent in the workroom.

We don't know everything about the future, but we do know three facts as Christians: First, Jesus will appear. Second, we shall be like Him. Third, we shall see Him as He is. John wrote, "But we know that when he appears, we shall be like him, for we shall see him as he is" (3:2).

One day we shall give an accounting before Jesus. Paul tells us, "At that time each will receive his praise from God" (1 Cor. 4:5). We are destined to be conformed to the image of God in Christ Jesus. We shall not only be with Jesus, but "we shall be like him."

Former pagans were translating a Bible lesson into their own language. When they came to 1 John 3:2, they read with astonishment: "But we know that when he appears, we shall be like him." That was beyond comprehension! They said to the Christian leader, "This is too much. Let us write instead that we shall be permitted to kiss His feet."

However, God is still at work: "We shall be like him." The best is yet to be. Think of it—the most exciting time of our lives is still ahead of us! Be patient—God isn't finished with us yet.

Jesus has been called "the great Believer in man." Common people heard Him gladly because He did not treat them as common people. He was always concerned for the least, the last, and the lost. And Jesus believes in you—whether you are a sinner, backslider, or struggling saint full of self-despisings. He sees you at this moment as the person you are capable of becoming through His grace. He sees the lonely path you have walked, the battles you have fought, the conflicts you have faced. And Jesus sees the great possibilities that lie in you and me.

In a builder's yard, Michelangelo, the sculptor, saw a lump of marble cast aside—stained, misshaped, unattractive. He said to the builder, "Let me have it. I'll take it to my studio. An angel is imprisoned in that marble, and I can set it free!"

That's how God feels about you. Go to the records. See how Jesus always reacted to people. Mary of Magdala was despised by people because she was a great sinner. Jesus didn't pretend she was an angel—but He could see the angel imprisoned in her and set it free! Jesus sees in us things we could never see in ourselves—for He sees the completed picture, the finished work of art.

We have reason to rejoice: "And we, who with unveiled faces all reflect the Lord's glory, are being transformed into his likeness with ever-increasing glory, which comes from the Lord, who is the Spirit" (2 Cor. 3:18).

10

He Breaks the Power of Canceled Sin

▽

1 JOHN 3:4-10

△

*W*HEN IS A person a thief? Does he have to steal first before he is a thief? Is he an honest man until he steals? Would an honest person steal? So, when does one become a thief?

I used to think a person became a thief when he stole something. Observing man's fallen nature and studying God's Word, I now understand man is a thief by his inner nature and disposition. If he was honest before he stole, he would never steal. Why does he steal? Because he is a thief. A person is not a sinner because he sins. He sins because he is a sinner. He has the disposition of rebellion.

The apostle John deals with this issue: "Dear children, do not let anyone lead you astray. He who does what is right is righteous, just as he [Jesus] is righteous" (v. 7). It sounds simple, but it's profound. Right living springs from a righteous inner nature. One doesn't do good things in order to be God's child; one becomes God's child by faith in order to do the right things.

In John's day Gnostics, the false teachers, taught that a Christian didn't need to be concerned about sin. Only his body could commit sin, for his spirit belonged to Christ. Thus, he could participate wholeheartedly in acts of sin. Gnostics believed that sin is natural and inherent to the physical body but did not affect the spirit. We know, however, that the body is neutral, governed either by a carnal spirit or a godly spirit.

Counterfeit Christians tried to convince believers that one could be "saved" and still practice sin. The apostle John responded with his written sermon: no one can practice sin without breaking God's law.

In 1976 Lyle Blackwood, professional football player, met a man who asked, "If you were to die right now, where would you spend eternity—heaven or hell?" Lyle was haunted by that question. The man explained that he was a sinner—the bad news—and he explained the Good News, too, that God is loving and just and provided Jesus Christ as a free gift for the forgiveness of sins.

At that time Lyle and his wife, Suzanne, received Christ as Savior. Suzanne began to grow spiritually, but Lyle still did not want to make Jesus the Lord of his life. He had not gotten serious with God yet. He learned the hard way that God had not taken away his capacity to sin, yet He *had* taken away his capacity to enjoy sin. Growing more and more miserable, Lyle learned that "you reap what you sow" (see Gal. 6:7). Sowing disobedience, he reaped guilt.

Lyle remembers, "I was torn up. God was convicting me about what I was doing." Finally he couldn't stand a life of sin any longer. At a Professional Athletes Outreach Conference he confessed, "I'm sick and tired of all this." God's Word helped him deal with sin in his life and gave him victory over it.

John shows us that the Lord "breaks the power of canceled sin."

I. GOD EXPOSES SIN

John tells us two things about sin.
First, sin is lawlessness or rebellion: "Everyone who

sins breaks the law; in fact, sin is lawlessness" (v. 4). That profound statement identifies human heartache and misery: behind human tragedy is a spirit of rebellion. The determination to please oneself at all costs has hurt more people than any other cause.

John emphasizes sin as an attitude of rebellion. Sins express the rebellious attitude. "Sin is lawlessness."

Sin is the demanding desire to have your own way, to become a law unto yourself, to make up your own rules for life, and to disregard the laws of life that already exist. Lawlessness is defiance. It deliberately climbs the fence posted "No Trespassing." In spite of warnings, we strut into forbidden fields. Sin as lawlessness is not ignorance, but intention. Lawlessness springs from hatred of God in the same way that obedience springs from our love for God.

By faith, the Christian has been born into the family of God. That He is love doesn't mean He has no rules and regulations for His family. His children find freedom in Christ—but His children are not lawless. Paul testified, "I am not free from God's law but am under Christ's law" (1 Cor. 9:21). Rebellion is not acceptable in God's children.

Second, sin is of the devil: "He who does what is sinful is of the devil, because the devil has been sinning from the beginning" (v. 8). If a person continues practicing sin, he is being led by the same one who led Adam and Eve into rebellion—Satan. We repeat the devil's sin when we adopt the attitude, "I'll do what I want. I am a law unto myself." That disposition caused Satan's fall from heaven from the beginning. Lawlessness acts without regard for any other law, any other person, or any other authority.

John tells us that God exposes sin for what it is—a rebellion led by the devil himself. If we offer the old excuse, "The devil made me do it!" the obvious question is, "Why are you listening to him?"

John was not including everything short of absolute perfection when he wrote, "He who does what is sinful is of the devil." As long as we live and breathe, we face limitations of human nature. A heart perfect toward God doesn't guarantee perfect judgment. Failures are not sin unless the motive is lawlessness and rebellion. In the Bible involuntary transgressions are called "faults." We should confess our faults and trust in Jesus, "who is able to keep you from falling and to present you before his glorious presence without fault and with great joy" (Jude 24).

Failures and faults make us question our commitment. We assume that if we had more faith we would be more Christlike. Some people try to resolve the conflict by accepting the idea, "Everybody sins every day in word, thought, and deed." Accepting that idea, they will act it out. The devil himself can't do worse than that—rebelling every day in word, thought, and deed.

John teaches victory over sin: "My dear children, I write this to you so that you will not sin. But if anybody does sin, we have one who speaks to the Father in our defense—Jesus Christ, the Righteous One" (1 John 2:1). In spite of failures and faults—even unexpected sin—we can walk in unbroken fellowship with Jesus.

II. GOD ERADICATES SIN

The holy life is not an option; it is the mark of belonging to Jesus Christ. God provided for us to experience and enjoy a life of holiness. John gives two reasons why Jesus came and died.

First, God sent Jesus to *take away our sins:* "But you know that he appeared so that he might take away our sins" (v. 5). The angel who announced Jesus' birth to Joseph said: "You are to give him the name Jesus, because he will save his people from their sins" (Matt. 1:21). When we take Jesus by faith, our past sins are canceled out. John rejoiced, "If we confess our sins, he is faithful and just and will forgive us our sins and purify us from all unrighteousness" (1 John 1:9).

Unconfessed sin is the first step in moving away from a close walk with Jesus. The Bible calls it "backsliding." God promised, "I will cure you of backsliding" (Jer. 3:22). He implies that "backsliding" resembles illness. First is the invasion of the body by a disease germ. Then infection follows. A gradual decline sets in: no pep, no appetite, no interest in normal activities. Then comes the collapse!

Spiritual decline follows the same course. First, sin invades with that spirit of rebellion. We yield to its influence, and infection sets in. A gradual decline follows. We lose our appetite for spiritual things. We become listless and irritable. Finally we experience spiritual collapse. The only remedy is to confess and forsake our sin and turn to Jesus for cleansing and wholeness.

An old man lived near the neighborhood church. The peculiar fellow would go out with a shopping bag and pick up junk out of trash cans. Every day he did the same thing. You can imagine what his house looked like inside. He left a narrow corridor running through the house so that you could walk through it, but it was stacked to the ceiling with bags of junk.

He was ordered by the fire department to clean out his house, or he would be fined or sent to jail. The pastor talked him into letting some people of the church come in and clean the house for him. He explained to the old man that if he didn't get it cleaned out, he would be in trouble with the fire department. The old man reluctantly agreed.

One day a crew from the church cleaned out the house and hauled three huge truckloads of junk to the dump.

The next day the old man picked up a bag and started all over again. The church people hadn't found a solution that reached his real problem—the man's inner nature.

God went beyond clearing out the junk of our unconfessed sins. He aimed at the source of our acts of sin—man's inner nature of sin.

Second, God sent Jesus to *destroy the devil's work:* "The reason the Son of God appeared was to destroy the devil's work" (v. 8). Jesus came to earth and took on himself our human nature in order to fix us up and present us to His Father in as good a condition as when we originally came from God's hand! Not only did Jesus come to break the power of sin over us, but also He came to destroy the nature of sin in us. By His sacrificial death, Jesus broke the power of our sinful nature. Charles Wesley exclaimed:

> *He breaks the power of canceled sin;*
> *He sets the prisoner free.*
> *His blood can make the foulest clean;*
> *His blood availed for me.*

"The Son of God appeared . . . to *destroy* the devil's work." The Greek word here for "to destroy" means "to loosen, unbind, dissolve, break up, destroy, annul, cancel, demolish, make void, nullify." These are tough words. God intends to eliminate the inner nature of rebellion—thus getting to the source of our sin.

Some people object to the idea of "eradication" of our sinful nature. They feel one can only suppress sin—hold it down and keep it under control. They can only conceive of a shoddy, once-over dusting off of a person's outer demeanor. But God's Word speaks of cleansing by the Holy Spirit in a way that sounds like the dictionary definition of "to eradicate": "To pull up by the roots; to destroy at the roots; to root out; as to eradicate weeds. To destroy thoroughly; to get rid of; to wipe out." That sounds thorough and complete to me!

Dr. Erwin Lutzer, pastor of Moody Memorial Church, wrote: "It is not enough simply to confess our sins if we want to be delivered from sin's power. We must go a step further and accept the fact that God also has a remedy for the sin nature within us. Confessing our sins is often like sawing branches off a tree; but if we do not want the tree to grow, it is more effective to strike at its roots. That is why God, the divine Surgeon, is not concerned only that we confess our sins; He goes directly for our hearts."[66]

God in Christ dealt a deathblow to the power of sin in our lives: "For we know that our old self was crucified with him so that the body of sin might be done away with" (Rom. 6:6).

Jesus came to "break the power of canceled sin": "The Son of God appeared . . . to destroy the devil's work." If Jesus cannot destroy the sin Satan planted in the heart, then the Bible is not true. If Jesus cannot destroy the sin Satan planted in the heart, then Jesus failed in His mission. If Jesus cannot destroy the sin Satan planted in the heart, then Satan is more powerful than Jesus. If Jesus cannot destroy the sin Satan planted in the heart, then we must sin—and without freedom to keep from sinning, we are not morally responsible. That makes nonsense out of Scripture! Jesus never rests until He has eliminated from your nature everything that is contrary to His nature!

III. GOD DISPLACES SIN

Nature abhors a vacuum. Darkness is the absence of light. A sinful heart is the absence of the Divine Presence. Though God has cleansed my heart, if I begin to quench the Holy Spirit, my old sinful self rushes back into the void—as darkness rushes in when light has been quenched. We need a divine filling to keep us clean!

To the person who thinks that sinning is an ongoing part of his Christian life, the Bible has a revolutionary word.

First, *the life of Christ gives no place to sin:* "And in him [Jesus] is no sin. No one who lives in him keeps on sinning" (vv. 5-6). As the believer opens his heart to the life of Christ and keeps in fellowship with Jesus, he desires ever more strongly to be like Him. Remaining in Christ, he does not go on sinning. John does not deny that Christians may sin; he denies that Christians can *live in sin*. The Christian can never be at peace with sin. He may slip and sin, but it's the exception, not the ruling principle of his heart and life.

Defeated Christians strive by self-effort to live a godly life. But I cannot do anything to make God love me more; I cannot do anything to make God love me less. The Christian must allow Christ to live in him.

Coming from the hospital on the day Ruth had surgery, I passed a neighborhood church. On their portable marquee was the biblical message about having your sins washed white as snow. Beneath that sign was the biggest pile of dirty snow I had ever seen!

I've thought of the contrast. In dealing with sin in their lives, some people would rather change the biblical message of cleansing from sin to "sinning every day in word, thought, and deed." I believe the apostle John is saying, "Change your claim or change your name!" If you don't want to quit sinning, then quit calling yourself "Christian." John adds, "No one who continues to sin has either seen him or known him" (v. 6).

If you are claiming to be a Christian, but you are not turning away from sin, if you are going on week after week, month after month, year after year in a sinful condition or sinful relationship that you know is wrong, then you are not a Christian. In spite of your religious experiences, in spite of your claim, in spite of your attendance in church, you have not been born again. No one who persists in sin belongs to Jesus Christ.

Second, *the nature of God has no room for sin:* "No one who is born of God will continue to sin, because God's seed remains in him; he cannot go on sinning, because he has been born of God" (v. 9).

The born again have been set free from habitual sin as a dominating force. God's holy nature displaces our sinful nature. The Bible refers to this experience as "sanctification." It does not prevent the believer from sinning, but it removes the Christian's inborn desire to sin. Sin is no longer natural to the believer. It is contrary to his inner nature. He cannot go on living in what he knows to be sin.

A sheep and a pig may both stumble into a mudhole. However, the difference in their natures occasions different responses. The pig is perfectly happy. He feels right at home. But the sheep is miserable and yearns to get out immediately. "No one . . . born of God will continue to sin, because God's seed remains in him; he cannot go on sinning, because he has been born of God." God's own nature within the believer begins to bring him to a spiritual maturity.

Being born of God, we have the power of God to stop sinning: "he cannot go on sinning." A saint cannot sin in the same way an honest man cannot steal or a truthful man cannot lie. Sinning is incompatible with being "born again." John is talking about habitual practice, not occasional lapse. John makes it clear that God's children are different from the devil's children in the fact that God's children quit their sins while the devil's children go on sinning: "This is how we know who the children of God are and who the children of the devil are: Anyone who does not do what is right is not a child of [the living] God" (v. 10).

People often imagine three classes of persons—the

children of the devil, the children of God, and then a vast group in between who are morally neutral, neither devilish nor divine. In fact, most people would classify themselves in the middle somewhere. But God says it isn't so. We are either children of God or children of the devil. Which are you?

Uncle Buddy Robinson said, "No man is a sinner saved by grace. If he is saved by grace, he is not a sinner. And if he is a sinner, he is not saved."

If we have been born again, soon after our conversion God's Spirit begins to put His finger on certain things in our lives and says, "These must go."

We usually react, "But they're such little things, Lord. They don't really matter. Let's not talk about these trivial things. Let's go on in our happy fellowship together—You and me, Jesus."

But those things are not minor. They have been keeping us in spiritual bondage. Because God loves us, He won't put up with them. Inflexibly He stands there asking, "What are you going to do about this?"

This passage in 1 John was not given so that we might check up on other people. God inspired these words so that we may examine ourselves. Is your heart right with God? Do you have God's nature residing within? Do you harbor unconfessed sin—and if so, are you willing to confess it to Jesus and forsake it forever?

God's grace is available as you surrender all to Him. The greatest miracle God performs today is to take an unholy man, make him holy, and keep him holy in an unholy world.

For a long time after World War II, Japanese troops hid in caves and jungles of the Pacific islands. These stragglers lived like frightened savages. They did not know the war was over. When someone finally convinced them that it was no longer necessary to fight, they surrendered at last—and accepted the peace they had long missed.

Christian friends, Satan is a defeated enemy. He may win a few skirmishes, but *he has already lost the war!* God has exposed sin. God destroys the nature of sin in those who are surrendered to Him. God awaits the opportunity to fill you with His Holy Spirit, delivering you from bondage to sin. You no longer need to live like a rebel. Jesus came to break "the power of canceled sin."

11

Love That Stoops

▽

1 JOHN 3:11-18

△

*L*OVE IS A Christian virtue—the "fruit of the Spirit" (Gal. 5:22).

The comic strip caveman, B. C., opens a box. A letter in the box says, "Congratulations! You have just purchased the world's finest fire-starting kit!" The next picture shows him reading on: "The flint is of the finest stone imported from the Orient. Your striker has been handcrafted by Old World craftsmen. The kindling has been carefully selected by screened lumberjacks. Your kit was packaged and inspected by little old grannies working in a dust-free environment, and your fire kit dealer has sworn an oath of devotion to customers."

In the next picture, B. C. is rubbing two sticks together. A cave woman asks, "What's with the sticks? Where is your new fire-starting kit?"

He looks up, smiles, and says, "I built a shrine around it."

Has the Church taken all the wonderful equipment God has given to us and made it into a shrine? Have we built shrines around God's kind of love?

I cut out an advertisement for church steeples from a religious magazine. The advertisement had emblazoned in big letters: "THE CROWNING GLORY OF YOUR

CHURCH." The glory of the church is *never* in steeples or buildings or preachers or musicians or programs. It is in the reflected glory of Jesus, who said, "Love one another. . . . all men will know that you are my disciples, if you love one another" (John 13:34-35).

Reformer John Knox said, "The [early] Christian community was not a memorial society with its eyes fastened on a departed master; it was a dynamic community created around a living and present Lord." God never intended for His people to build a shrine around love. Thus, John wrote, "This is the message you heard from the beginning: We should love one another" (v. 11).

Someone gave me a handwritten note: "Love that goes upward, from the heart of man to God, is adoration. Love that goes outward, from one heart to another, is affection. But love that stoops is grace." That's the kind of love that John describes in 1 John 3:11-18—"Love that stoops."

I. LOVE THAT STOOPS
PROVES NEW LIFE IN CHRIST

John wrote to combat the Gnostics, who believed that life in the Spirit was obtained by secret knowledge. The Greek word *gnosis*, "to know," gave the Gnostics their name. Knowledge was their key word. John did not reject knowledge; he used the word "know" 36 times in 1 John. But his dominant theme was the word "love"; he used it 43 times. To know was good, but to love was best!

John contrasts love with hatred: "Do not be like Cain, who belonged to the evil one and murdered his brother. [literally, "cut his brother's throat" (JB) or "butchered his brother" (Williams)]. And why did he murder him? Because his own actions were evil and his brother's were righteous" (v. 12). As this incident vividly illustrates, the schism between the two brothers—Cain and Abel—centered in religious differences. In Genesis 4, Cain is not an atheist, but a worshiper bringing sacrifice to God. The real test is not a religious ceremony, but love for one's brother. Cain resented his brother's righteousness before God—the same kind of envy that drove the Jewish priests to demand Jesus' death on the Cross.

No wonder John wrote, "Do not be surprised, my brothers, if the world hates you" (v. 13). The more Christlike you become, the more the world around you will hate and hiss at you! Our world resents righteousness and would destroy those who expose its unrighteousness. A good man's life rebukes the way of an evil person.

Socrates embodied goodness. One of his peers—brilliant, erratic, debauched, wild, and reckless—said to him, "Socrates, I hate you, because every time I meet you, you show me what I am."

As people persecute Christians by various degrees, they attempt to conceal their antagonism for Jesus. The individual Christian merely becomes the target for people's animosity toward goodness. As Paul witnessed, "We are hard pressed on every side, but not crushed; perplexed, but not in despair; persecuted, but not abandoned; struck down, but not destroyed" (2 Cor. 4:8-9).

Continuing his contrast between hatred and love, John writes, "Anyone who hates his brother is a murderer, and you know that no murderer has eternal life in him" (v. 15). Hatred is sin. The question is not, "What did I do?" but "What did I *want* to do? What would I have done if I were free to do as I please?"

That's why Jesus equates attitude with the deed. Your attitude portrays what you really are if uninhibited and unrestrained by fear of consequences. Hatred is murder in embryo form.

John's point is that hatred is incompatible with the Christian life. God does not dwell in the heart filled with hatred. New life in Christ is proved by a loved that stoops to human need: "We know that we have passed from death to life, because we love our brothers. Anyone who does not love remains in death" (v. 14). Love for our brothers is the indispensable sign of our conversion to Jesus Christ. When I see a bird that looks like a duck, quacks like a duck, has webbed feet like a duck, paddles in the water like a duck, and prefers the company of ducks, I can't resist the conclusion that it must be a duck. "Birds of a feather flock together." We gravitate to what lures us most. We eventually show up where we belong. "We know that we have passed from death to life, because we love our brothers." If we don't love the brethren, we belong to the other crowd. Christians "have passed from death to life"—it sounds something like a resurrection! No one grows into becoming a Christian. It takes a divine, spiritual re-creation. God plants spiritual life into a person who has been spiritually dead. Love proves that new life has indeed been given. Without love, we are "nothing" (1 Cor. 13:2).

Spiritual life does not come by loving our brothers, but love for our brothers gives evidence of spiritual life. Jesus said, "I tell you the truth, whoever hears my word and believes him who sent me has eternal life and will not be condemned; he has crossed over from death to life" (John 5:24). Love for one's brothers proves the possession of eternal life. That's why it seems so strange to see people or groups who profess Christianity fighting and fussing between themselves. A person out of sorts with fellow Christians is out of sorts with God and himself.

We prove our love by doing good to our brothers. Isaiah wrote, "Stop doing wrong, learn to do right!" (1:16-17). J. B. Phillips paraphrased 1 Cor. 13:4, "This love of which I speak . . . looks for a way of being constructive." Our love for God is measured by our love for the brother we least like!

In an old, yellowed *Hutchings California Magazine* printed in 1860 was a story of two brothers traveling in Lapland. On a bitter, freezing day they were traveling in a sled, wrapped in furs from head to foot—yet nearly frozen. Along the way, they found a lone traveler numb and dying in the snow. One of the brothers said, "Let's stop and help. We must save his life."

The other brother argued, "We'll lose our own lives if we stop. No one but a fool would think of stopping on a day like this. I wouldn't give my cloak to save a hundred travelers!"

Said the first brother, "I can't see this stranger die. I must go help him." With great effort he wrapped the stranger in one of his furs and struggled, carrying him on his back. Nearly exhausted, he caught up with the sled. He called out, "Brother, look! I have saved this man's life— and I think my own. I'm almost hot with exhaustion."

But his brother did not answer. He was sitting in his furs on the sled, frozen to death. "Anyone who does not love remains in death."

II. LOVE THAT STOOPS
PATTERNS AFTER JESUS

The English word "love" has been so abused, debased, and diluted that nearly everyone claims to love by his own definition. John defines his idea of love: "This is how we know what love is: Jesus Christ laid down his life for us" (v. 16). His word for "love" is the Greek word *agapē*. It is a love that stoops, that goes to work—with or without emotions. Most people define love in emotional terms: "For

God so loved the world that He sat in heaven and had warm feelings!" Nonsense! God so loved the world that He gave—a volitional commitment that stands firm when emotions fade.

Did you know that the Bible has two John 3:16s? Most Christians memorize John 3:16—"For God so loved the world, that he gave his only begotten Son, that whosoever believeth in him should not perish, but have everlasting life" (KJV). Those powerful words are important words. We cherish them. But how many Christians memorize 1 John 3:16? "This is how we know what love is: Jesus Christ laid down his life for us. And we ought to lay down our lives for our brothers." These words tell the same story of love's sacrifice—Jesus giving himself for us. Both verses have almost the same number of words, but we have taken to one and not the other. First John 3:16 is seldom quoted. Why?

In John 3:16 God does everything, and we have only to *believe*. We like that! However, in 1 John 3:16, God does His part—"Jesus Christ laid down his life for us"—and then we are commanded to do our part: "And we ought to lay down our lives for our brothers." That comes as quite a shock. That last part is not so popular. We would rather emphasize what God is doing than get involved—in what we should be doing.

In the Book of Acts, early Christians practiced two kinds of breaking of bread: the Love Feast, or breaking of common bread in daily fellowship; and the Lord's Supper, or breaking of Communion bread. In the Book of Acts, the breaking of common bread in fellowship was the most prominent one. As the years passed by, the bread of Holy Communion gradually took the place of prominence. Why?

Breaking the bread of Holy Communion commemorated what Jesus did in laying down His life for us. Breaking of common bread in daily fellowship emphasized our responsibility to love and share with our brothers in Christ. Gradually the idea of what we should do for others was dropped, and Christians preferred to celebrate only what Jesus did for us. People prefer to turn religion into rites and ceremonies instead of acts of service. We prefer to build a shrine around "love."

To understand a love that stoops, let's hear again what Jesus did: "Jesus Christ laid down his life for us." Only John's writings use the words "laid down his life." It comes from a Greek word that means "to place" or "to put aside." It implies "laying aside something—laying aside one's clothes, divesting oneself of something." In John 13:4 it describes Jesus laying aside His outer garment to stoop down and wash His disciples' feet. In what became an early Christian hymn, Paul describes Jesus, "Who, being in very nature God, did not consider equality with God something to be grasped, but made himself nothing, taking the very nature of a servant, being made in human likeness. And being found in appearance as a man, he humbled himself and became obedient to death—even death on a cross!" (Phil. 2:6-8). That's love that stoops all the way to our deepest need!

Here's the unpopular part: "And we ought to lay down our lives for our brothers." The Greek grammar suggests a present, ongoing, continuous laying down of our lives for one another. We are seldom called upon to *die* for another, but we need to learn how to *live* for one another. Love that stoops voluntarily surrenders its rights in order to minister to another person. This love stoops to do anything for another's benefit. What are you prepared to "lay down"?

John Henry Jowett wrote, "There is much spurious love about. It lays nothing down; it only takes things up! It is self-seeking, using the speech and accents of love. It is a 'work of the flesh' which has stolen the label of a 'fruit of the Spirit.' Love may always be known by its expenditures."

The first law of physical life is self-preservation. The Bible teaches us that self-sacrifice is the first law of spiritual life.

Reuben Welch said of 1 John 3:16:

> I think I know a little bit about what it means to hold [life] back . . . Sometimes I wonder what we are saving ourselves for . . . We want to save ourselves, and keep ourselves and hold ourselves back as though the highest goal in life would be to look good in our caskets. It's no special blessing to come to the end of life with love unshared, selves ungiven, activities unactivated, deeds undone, emotions unextended . . . I have the feeling that when a person is middle-aged, he ought to be about half used up . . . What am I saving myself for?[67]

Our local newspaper had an article titled "Birmingham Samaritan Found Dead." Willie Perry had been known around Birmingham, Ala., for driving his "Rescue Ship," a 1971 Thunderbird equipped with flashing yellow and red lights. He always stopped to help stranded motorists.

He was found dead in his garage from accidental carbon monoxide poisoning. The mayor said, "Perry was a very special blessing to the city of Birmingham. He was one of the few people who disregarded himself completely in the name of others."

That's a good definition of love that stoops.

III. LOVE THAT STOOPS CALLS TO ACTION

John lets us down with a thump in his next sentence: "If anyone has material possessions and sees his brother in need but has no pity on him, how can the love of God be in him?" (v. 17). We readily consent to the high ideal of laying down one's life—that is a remote possibility, so we can get enthused about it. We would be content to wait for that unlikely moment that calls for martydom and live our present comfortable life undisturbed. But John brings us to reality: "If anyone has material possessions and sees his brother in need."

If we are going to help our brother, we must meet three conditions.

First, *we must have enough to meet our brother's need.* Dr. E. V. Hill of Los Angeles said, "When God blesses you materially, He seldom has you in mind. God gives it to you so that He can get it through you. If He can't get it through you, He'll stop giving it to you!"

Second, *we must care enough to know our brother's need exists.* John moved from loving "our brothers" in the plural to loving "his brother" in the singular. It's a lot easier to get excited about "humanity" than to love that person you know who's so uninteresting, exasperating, or irritating. C. S. Lewis noted, "Loving everybody in general may be an excuse for loving nobody in particular."

That's the point of Jesus' parable of the Good Samaritan. The lawyer came to Jesus wanting to debate an abstract idea: "Who is my neighbor?" (Luke 10:29).

But Jesus focused on one man in desperate need: To whom can I be a neighbor?

Many people refuse to do anything since they can't do everything. Because they can't set the world on fire, they won't light a candle. Because they can't save the world, they refuse to save a brother in need.

Third, *we must love enough to share with our brother.* Notice how practical the Bible gets: "Suppose a brother or sister is without clothes and daily food. If one of you says to him, 'Go, I wish you well; keep warm and well fed,' but does nothing about his physical needs, what good is it?" (James 2:15-16).

John has an interesting phrase, "but has no pity on him" (v. 17). The Greek idea suggests "close up [our] insides against him." If we try to protect ourselves from feeling our brother's need inside, "how can the love of God be in" us? God opened His great heart of love and compassion for us. How can we settle for closing our hearts against our brother?

"Dear children, let us not love with words or tongue but with actions and in truth" (v. 18). Let's resist the temptation to be superficial in love. Let's do more than talk about a need; let's love "in deed"—let's *do* something! Barclay noted, "Fine words will never take the place of fine deeds; and not all the talk of Christian love in the world will take the place of a kindly action to a man in need, made at the expense of some self-denial and some self-sacrifice, for in that action the principle of the Cross is operative again."[68] An act of love opens people's hearts to hear our words of love.

People are just like us. People hurt in the same ways we hurt. We can be God's answer to one another within the fellowship of God's family: "love . . . with actions and in truth." "Love" is not simply a word to write on a wall plaque. "Love" is what we do to people who irritate us, when we are upset and angry and feel like striking back. "Little children, let us stop just *saying* we love people; let us *really* love them, and *show it* by our *actions*" (v. 18, TLB).

As brothers and sisters, we love one another at first sight because we are Christians; and then we move toward getting acquainted. Out in the world, people first get acquainted; and then move cautiously into love—sometimes. Even the skeptical philosopher, Bertrand Russell, said, "Of all forms of caution, caution in love is perhaps the most fatal to human happiness." As a result, most people have many acquaintances and only a few friends—but they are dying from a lack of love.

Would you begin to love one another with a love that stoops and lifts in Jesus' name?

12

Begin a New Past

▽

1 JOHN 3:19-24

△

A YOUNG BOY HELPED his dad plant a tree. One day his dad found him holding the little tree in his hand, having pulled it up by the roots. Startled, the father asked, "What are you doing?"

The boy replied, "I was trying to find out if it was growing!"

In Christian experience "introspection destroys emotion." When we start taking ourselves apart, continually investigating ourselves to see if we are still children of God, we eventually fall into confusion. Sometimes, in fact, we forfeit the joy of the Lord by trying too hard to have an emotional "high" all the time. We form a discipleship that says, "Lord, I'll serve You if You will make me feel good."

Life conditions us to be hard on ourselves. We can eloquently recite our liabilities, but we can stammer over our assets. Past failures haunt our memories. Missed opportunities cloud today's open doors. A vague uneasiness hints of an undetermined sense of guilt or self-condemnation. The Christian may begin to doubt himself, uncertain that he belongs to God. Doubt hinders his fellowship with God and handicaps his service to others.

If you are not sure you belong, you don't feel comfortable in God's presence—and prayer is stifled. Feeling unfit, you have no real confidence that God hears your prayers. A "condemning heart" or an "accusing conscience" robs your peace of mind. Jeremiah must have felt those false accusations of his heart: "The heart is deceitful above all things and beyond cure. Who can understand it? 'I the Lord search the heart and examine the mind'" (17:9-10). Thank God, He knows the heart!

Having a pastor's heart, John deals with this question that sometimes plagues sincere Christians. John begins and ends this paragraph with the words, "This is how we know." He pauses to talk about assurance in the believer's heart. John wishes to bring healing to the wounded conscience, not to open the wounds wider. We do not need to dump more guilt on each other, but to encourage each Christian to really believe God's estimate of him.

A poster hanging on the wall of an Alcoholics Anonymous meeting room should excite us: "Begin a new past!" As Lloyd Ogilvie said, "We don't have to go on collecting bad memories."

When we suffer from self-condemnation, John points us to God's avenues of assurance.

I. GOD REASSURES THROUGH HIS INTIMATE KNOWLEDGE

Having described "love that stoops," John says, "This then is how we know that we belong to the truth, and how we set our hearts at rest in his presence whenever our hearts condemn us. For God is greater than our hearts, and he knows everything" (vv. 19-20).

An accusing or guilty conscience springs from one of three causes. First, our heart may condemn us when we have committed sin: something we know is wrong. Second, our heart may condemn us when we have been ignored, misunderstood, or mistreated: something that makes us wonder if we are worthy in God's sight. Third, our heart may condemn us when we have been inactive in Christian service: something that makes us feel useless. In each case, the enemy is quick to stir up a sense of condemnation. He makes us question our relationship with Jesus.

John says that our acts of love to one another give proof that we belong to God: "This then is how we know that we belong to the truth." If the Christian has sinned, he has immediate access to Jesus for forgiveness as he confesses his sin. If he feels unworthy or useless, his love for the brothers is evidence that he is in Christ—in spite of self-condemnation. Paul rejoices with us, "Therefore, there is now no condemnation for those who are in Christ Jesus" (Rom. 8:1). Our self-doubts are silenced by self-giving and self-sacrificing love for one another. It is proof that God is at work in us. We belong to Him.

Though we are under the cloud of self-condemnation, our acts of love "set our hearts at rest in his presence." The phrase "set our hearts at rest" can mean "assure" or "tranquilize." The overactive "accusing heart" can be tranquilized or assured—quieted before the Lord. When we love as Jesus loved, we demonstrate His character and show that we belong to Him—in spite of our self-condemnation.

Ray Stedman visited Vietnam before the outbreak of war. He spoke to a conference of about 300 pastors through interpreters. A pastor came to him in private and poured out a tale of distress. He felt he had been mistreated by his fellow pastors, cut out of an office he felt should have been his. Deeply disturbed over it, the pastor felt he should ask for a full airing of the conflict with all the other pastors at the conference.

Turning to Phil. 2:5-8, Stedman read via an interpreter: "Your attitude should be the same as that of Christ Jesus:

Who, being in very nature God, did not consider equality with God something to be grasped, but made himself nothing, taking the very nature of a servant, being made in human likeness. And being found in appearance as a man, he humbled himself and became obedient to death—even death on a cross!" Then the American visitor suggested the pastor forget the whole matter.

The pastor was not yet receptive, but during the conference God's Spirit went to work on him. At the conclusion of the conference, he came to Stedman and said, "You were right. God has been dealing with my heart. It was only to justify myself that I was thinking all these things. God has helped me put the whole matter aside. What joy and peace are mine now."

Stedman commented, "That is exactly what John is talking about. By this response of genuine self-giving love to another who has injured us we prove to ourselves that we are of the truth and thus reassure our condemning hearts."[69]

The Greek New Testament comes to us without punctuation. I believe John intended for verse 20 to read: "Whenever our hearts condemn us, God is greater than our hearts." The word "condemn" means literally "to know something held against us." Based on our past performance, we get a feeling of distrust toward ourselves—but "God is greater than our hearts." The devil would rob us of confidence. If there is sin, confess it and never let it accuse you again—on the basis of God's promise. While we should not treat sin lightly, we must not be harder on ourselves than God is: "God is greater than our hearts." He looks beyond our faults and sees our need: "If God is for us, who can be against us?" (Rom. 8:31).

John adds, "And he knows everything." When we are down on ourselves, God is up on the facts! Don't be despondent with yourself. Assurance of our sonship does not rest on our feelings, but on the fact of God's faithfulness. "He knows everything." He knows us better than we know ourselves. God has acquitted us—and His judgment is trustworthy.

Having denied Jesus three times, Peter was filled with remorse and wept bitterly. But Jesus knew everything. Peter's heart condemned him, but the Lord gave Peter the assurance he needed. Yes, Jesus knows our failures, but He also knows our love, our longings, our deep desire to serve Him.

Thomas à Kempis said, "Man sees the deed, but God knows the intention." God is not frustrated by our past performance. He's the Lord of the future. An old French proverb says, "To know all is to forgive all." "And He knows everything."

Would you reach out and trust God's love in spite of your self-doubt? God reassures through His intimate knowledge.

II. GOD REASSURES THROUGH HIS ANSWERS TO PRAYER

John continues his focus on assurance: "Dear friends, if our hearts do not condemn us, we have confidence before God and receive from him anything we ask" (vv. 21-22). In other words, if we have no unconfessed sin in our hearts, we have every reason to trust God's assessment of us as His children.

"We have confidence before God." Having exercised love for one another, we have proof that we are God's children. This same Greek word for "confidence" or "boldness" appears in Acts 4:13—"When they saw the *courage* ["boldness," KJV] of Peter and John and realized that they were unschooled, ordinary men, they were astonished and they took note that these men had been with Jesus." Ogilvie noted: "Boldness is the result of being with Jesus." He gives us the certainty of assurance, an unlimited welcome as His children before the throne of God. No longer do we need to limp before the Lord in prodigal's rags or beg with uncertainty as foreigners to God. With confidence we can take hold of what He has guaranteed. We honor God when we come boldly to His throne. With confidence, "Present your requests to God. And the peace of God . . . will guard your hearts and your minds in Christ Jesus" (Phil. 4:6-7).

Someone asked an African how he knew he was a child of God. He replied, "A cool breeze is blowing through my heart." Confidently expose yourselves to God's promises, and let their cool breezes blow through your hearts!

John says boldly, "We have confidence before God and *receive* from him anything we ask." His emphasis is not just on asking, but upon receiving—upon God's grace, God's goodness, and God's glory! John has put the verbs "receive" and "ask" in the present tense, meaning that receiving and asking are the believer's habit pattern. It's not a one-shot thing but a way of life. We are guaranteed an answer—it may be what we expect or something better. Our first self-defeating reaction is to explain away the promise.

John attached two conditions to that statement: "[We] receive from him anything we ask, because we obey his commandments and do what pleases him" (v. 22). Remember the admonition: "When all else fails, follow directions."

Again, the words "obey" and "do" are put in the present tense, suggesting obedience as a habit or a way of life. The more we bring Jesus into our lives and the more we are obedient to His ways, the more our requests will be in accord with His will. The more a child understands his father and his father's values, the more he knows how to ask and what to ask for. The more we know about God's character, the more effective is our asking according to our Heavenly Father's will.

Dr. Wiersbe wrote, "A Christian who lives to please God will discover that God finds ways to please His child. 'Delight thyself also in the Lord; and he shall give thee the desires of thine heart' (Ps. 37:4, KJV). When our *delight* is in the love of God, our *desires* will be in the will of God."[70]

Jesus says, "If you love me, you will obey what I command" (John 14:15). John gives us the content of obedience: "And this is his command: to believe in the name of his Son, Jesus Christ, and to love one another as he commanded us" (v. 23).

John introduces the word "believe" *(pisteuō)* for the first time in 1 John. More than simply giving mental assent, "believe" means "to put our weight down" upon God's faithfulness. *Pisteuō* is rooted in the Old Testament idea of faith. Faith is our response to the evidence of God's faithfulness. This kind of believing is more than a way of thinking; it is a way of living. You can put your weight down on God's character. He is worthy of our trust!

John's point is this: love for people proves that we are living in God's will where God can answer our prayers. Failure to love short-circuits our prayers. The Bible illustrates: "Husbands . . . be considerate as you live with your wives, and treat them with respect as the weaker partner and as heirs with you of the gracious gift of life, so that nothing will hinder your prayers" (1 Pet. 3:7).

Our beliefs and our actions of love go together. Christian theology and Christian ethics can never be divorced. Paul gave a classic definition of Christianity: "For in Christ

. . . [t]he only thing that counts is faith expressing itself through love" (Gal. 5:6).

One Christmas Eve when Norman Vincent Peale was 10 years old, he and his preacher father were passing a department store in Cincinnati. A dirty old fellow in a tattered coat took hold of Norman's sleeve and said, "Young man, give me something."

Repulsed, Norman pulled away, gave the man a slight push, and walked on indignantly. His father stopped. "You shouldn't treat a man like that—Christmas Eve or any other time."

"But, Dad, he's a bum."

"There is no such thing as a bum, Norman. There are many people who haven't made the most of their lives, but all of us are still loved by God!" Then the preacher took out his skinny old wallet and handed his son a dollar. "You catch up with that man. Tell him, 'Sir, I give you this dollar in the name of Jesus. Merry Christmas.'"

"Oh, no," Norman recoiled. "I can't do that."

"You do as I tell you, boy."

Chasing after the old tramp, Norman announced, "Sir, I give you this dollar in the name of Jesus. Merry Christmas."

The old fellow was shocked. He doffed his beat-up old cap and bowed to the boy. "I thank you, young sir. Merry Christmas."

Norman remembered, "In that moment, his face became beautiful to me. He was no longer a bum . . . 'Love one another,' Jesus said. No ifs . . . No reservations. And that's how Jesus loved. He loved the poor, the diseased, the prostitutes, the criminals, the 'bums.' He loved those who ridiculed, hated, and abused Him . . . You'll never grow taller, nor wiser, nor more beautiful than when you're putting those three words to work. 'Love one another.'"

III. GOD REASSURES THROUGH
HIS INDWELLING SPIRIT

"Those who obey his commands live in him, and he in them. And this is how we know that he lives in us: We know it by the Spirit he gave us" (v. 24).

For the first time in 1 John, the Holy Spirit is mentioned by name. Here's John's logic: an act of Christian love (1) reassures a doubting or self-condemned heart, (2) gives boldness to talk before God and get results, and (3) gives evidence of a Spirit-filled life. When a Christian obeys God by loving others, the indwelling Holy Spirit gives him a sense of confidence and assurance.

Jesus had promised His disciples at the Last Supper, "I will ask the Father, and he will give you another Counselor to be with you forever—the Spirit of truth" (John 14:16-17). Our assurance is based on truth revealed by the Spirit within.

When we have the Spirit and the Spirit has us, we can be assured of safety and security. Reassured in spite of our self-accusations, we know we are of the truth. We belong to God. We give ourselves fully to life in the Spirit. When you doubt, remember that the Holy Spirit dwells within you. He does not abandon you when you feel self-condemnation. Don't look at your failures. We all have them. Look at those acts of love the Holy Spirit has prompted and enabled you to perform—often in spite of your feelings.

C. W. Ruth declared, "You need not go outside and light a candle to see if the sun has risen." And the witness of the Spirit needs no secondhand confirmation. Peter testified, "God, who knows the heart, showed that he accepted them by giving the Holy Spirit to them, just as he did to us" (Acts 15:8).

If you have been condemning yourself, "Begin a new

past." Take God's word for it. No matter how much your heart may condemn you, put your confidence in the Lord. He still holds us in His hand: "The Lord knows those who are his" (2 Tim. 2:19).

The voice of temptation seeks to erode our relationship with God, to make us feel so bad about our failures that we conclude, "It's no use!" The temptation to despair would draw us *away* from God's love and truth. However, the voice of the Spirit would convict us of moral wrong in order to draw us *toward* God's love and truth. He assures us of God's love and acceptance.

When we feel like rejects and failures, we see the beckoning hand of Jesus: "I have chosen you" (John 15:16, KJV). What a relief to know that our Captain has *chosen* us, that we were not grudgingly taken after there was no one left to choose. Even before we chose Him, He made His selection: "I have chosen you." We are not rejects, but children of God! Even though He knows the worst about us, He still cares and loves us.

A college youth became so rebellious and wayward that his family and friends predicted he would go bad. Filled with resentment, he determined to live up to their expectations.

But one night, as he crept upstairs to his bedroom in the darkness, a door in the hallway opened. His grandmother stood there with a lighted candle for him. She put her hand on his shoulder and said five words that changed his life: "John, I believe in you."

In the darkness of that night, God brought a miracle of grace to his heart. He became a gifted preacher—traceable to those five words: "John, I believe in you."

13

Love Is Not Blind

▽

1 JOHN 4:1-6

△

*R*EPEATEDLY JOHN CLOSES a section of thought by dangling a new idea in front of us in the last sentence. Then he picks up the new idea and develops it.

In the previous section, 3:19-24, John dangles the thought: "And this is how we know that he lives in us: We know it by the Spirit he gave us" (v. 24). Then John warns, "Dear friends, do not believe every spirit, but test the spirits to see whether they are from God" (4:1).

Dr. Len Broughton concluded his sermon. After the benediction a man approached him and said, "As you preached, the Holy Spirit whispered in my ear and told me to ask you for $500, because I don't have $500."

"Do not believe every spirit, but test the spirits to see whether they are from God." Things can go from the humorous to the bizarre. Zena Hochman was charged with homicide in New York City. She had pushed another woman into the path of an oncoming subway train. Zena told reporters that she had "heard an inner voice direct her to push Mrs. Newman in front of the train."

Responses to inner guidance are useless if we're not sure the Spirit of God is bearing witness. John's warning to test the spirits is like a parenthesis in the middle of John's discourse on love. In fact, this warning to critically examine religious teachers precedes John's most powerful words on love. Why?

False movements and counterfeit religious teachers usually emphasize love, preying on people's unfulfilled need for love. Ray Stedman pointed out, "Every cult, every deviant group, every false movement makes its appeal in the name of love. No word in our language is capable of being stretched in so many directions as this word *love*."[71] He continues:

Is that not what we see in the Garden of Eden? The devil comes to Eve and says, "Is it really true that God is so harsh, so difficult, so unloving toward you that He has forbidden you to eat the fruit of the tree? . . . I think more of you than that. I'd never do anything like that to you. Could God actually say a thing like that and be a God of love? . . . If you eat of this fruit you will discover wonderful things. You will become as gods. You will enter a wonderful world that you've never dreamed of before. You will discover the thing you were made for, from which God is trying to keep you. As your friend, as your counselor, I suggest you hold back no longer. Take of the fruit and eat it." Does that not sound familiar? That is exactly the line that cults, isms, and schisms are using everywhere today. "If you really want to *live*, try what we have in stock."[72]

John was writing before the full and final revelation of the New Testament was in the hands of the Early Church. Without the Bible as we know it, the churches were dependent on preachers with inspired insight. What a perfect setting for false teachers and counterfeit Christians! Some were led astray as they sought to reinterpret Christianity in a form the world would find acceptable—a Christ without a Cross, a Jesus who was only a man.

Yes, believers are to love one another—but John warns, "Love is not blind!" John gives a threefold admonition to unsuspecting believers.

I. DON'T BE NAIVE: TRUTH STANDS UP UNDER SCRUTINY

John begins this parenthetical section, "Dear friends." Addressing them tenderly, he reminds his readers that what follows is very important. "Dear friends, do not believe every spirit, but test the spirits to see whether they are from God" (v. 1).

John makes a call for healthy skepticism: "Do not believe every spirit." The Gnostics perverted truth under the disguise of enlightenment as do modernistic liberals in our day. Every truth has its counterfeits. John Stott wrote, "There is urgent need . . . for discernment among Christians. We are often too gullible, and exhibit a naive readiness to credit messages and teaching which purport to come from the spirit world. There is such a thing, however, as a misguided charity and tolerance towards false doctrine."[73] Tolerance of error is often godless indifference. If a person has no convictions of right and wrong, he tolerates everything. Believing nothing, he falls for anything.

The apostle John encourages a biblical balance— avoiding the extreme naïveté that believes everything and the extreme suspicion that believes nothing. "Do not believe every *spirit*." The Greek word for spirit *(pneuma)* literally means "wind." John is counseling the believers to test the various winds of teaching blowing across their generation. Paul admonished, "Then we will no longer be infants . . . blown here and there by every wind of teaching" (Eph. 4:14).

John calls for the ring of truth: "Test the spirits to see whether they are from God." The purpose of examination was to discover whether or not the person or teaching rang true. John urges believers to explore the true and the good, not to collect garbage. Some people focus so much on ferreting out the false and the bad, they have lost their appetite for the true and the good.

"Test the spirits to see whether they are from God." The Greek word for "test" is rooted in the idea of "to think, to examine closely" *(dokeō)*. Paul uses the word in Rom. 12:2—"Then you will be able to *test* and *approve* what God's will is—his good, pleasing and perfect will." Again, Paul says, "We speak as men *approved* by God to be entrusted with the gospel" (1 Thess. 2:4, all italics added). If someone offered you a load of ore claiming it to be gold, you would be foolish to pay for it before you took it to an assay office and had it tested. In the days of John and Paul, metals and coins were constantly weighed and tested before being accepted. They weren't looking for counterfeits, of which there were many, but for coins that rang true.

This same word for "test" became the technical term for scrutinizing persons for public office. John is saying, "Apply the same effort to religious teachers and teachings. Truth will stand up under the test." This admonition calls us to use our heads and to check out what is being taught today. No Christian benefits from ignorance or sloppy thinking. We need to be wide-awake and eager to grow spiritually and intellectually.

The test, however, is not our limited human reason. The mind of man is not the ultimate authority. We drift into error when we forget that Jesus Christ is our Authority. When presenting our Christian faith, we should persuade people to accept Jesus Christ as their living Lord. When people come into a personal relationship with Him, they discover that He transforms, He delivers, He lives within. Quite naturally, they will come to accept the authority of Scripture. "Trust in the Lord with all your heart and lean not on your own understanding" (Prov. 3:5).

I test the spirits to see whether or not they are *from God (ek tou theou)*. Six times in these six verses, John uses this common Greek preposition "from God." It suggests a person, or a spirit, or a quality has its *source* and *origin in God*. When a believer is born again, he has his *source* and *origin in God*. So test the spirits to see if their sources are in God. The Bible says, "If what a prophet proclaims in the name of the Lord does not take place or come true, that is a message the Lord has not spoken. That prophet has spoken presumptuously. Do not be afraid of him" (Deut. 18:22).

Thomas Beverly, rector of Lilley, in Hertfordshire, England, had published a book in 1965 predicting that the world would end in 1967. In 1968 he wrote a book explaining that the world had ended in 1967, but no one paid any attention to it.[74]

Hindsight eloquently pronounced him false. But how are we to test religious teachers and religious teachings in the present moment?

II. DON'T COMPROMISE: BE SURE YOUR JESUS IS THE REAL JESUS

"This is how you can recognize the Spirit of God: Every spirit that acknowledges that Jesus Christ has come in the flesh is from God" (v. 2).

If a person claims to believe in Jesus, examine whether or not his Jesus is the real Jesus. People can fashion a "Jesus" after their own likes and dislikes, leaving out the Bible's announcement of Him.

Anthony Campolo says:

> Time and time again I am confronted by students in the university setting who say, "I don't believe in God. I used to, but I don't believe any more." I respond by saying, "Describe for me this God you don't believe in." And they can

138

do that with great precision. They sit there and describe exactly what this god is like that they have rejected.

When they finish, I smile and say, "Terrific! If that's what you've rejected, welcome to the club. I've rejected that god, too. Your problem is this: You've never met the living Lord of Scripture. You've never met the resurrected Jesus. You have been brought up in a church tradition that has had you worshipping a Jesus who is in fact a distortion, a Jesus who comes across as nothing more than an incarnation of the American value system."[75]

What "Jesus" is John talking about? The key to John's description is in his Gospel: "The Word was made flesh, and dwelt among us" (1:14, KJV). He wrote his Gospel to show that Jesus Christ is God. He wrote 1 John to show that Jesus Christ is also man. The Gospel of John proves the deity of Christ; 1 John proves the humanity of Christ. John's Gospel was written to convince Jews that Jesus is coequal and coeternal with God the Father; 1 John was written to convince Gentiles that Jesus is indeed human.

In Christian teaching, the word *Trinity* is important. *Trinity* is a combination of *tri,* meaning "three," and *unity,* meaning "one." A *trinity* is a three-in-one. Though the word *Trinity* does not appear in the Bible, the truth of it appears there. John here refers to God the Father, God the Son, and God the Holy Spirit: "Spirit of God . . . Jesus Christ . . . God" (v. 2). No person of the Trinity is expendable. John had written, "No one who denies the Son has the Father; whoever acknowledges the Son has the Father also" (1 John 2:23).

Probably the best translation of the Greek grammar is this: "Every spirit who is confessing Jesus as Christ come in the flesh is of God."[76] The acid test is, "Does this person or this movement confess Jesus as Christ come in the flesh?" Confession is more than what a person says. In the

Gospels, evil and unclean spirits recognized the deity of Jesus, but they did not "confess Christ." One's confession is also his practice or his actions. One's confession is his commitment. You say you believe in Jesus. Do you follow Him? Are you committed to Him? Is He Lord of your life?

Some people answer, "Yes, we believe in Jesus as Christ come in the flesh. It's written in our creed. We sing it in our hymnbooks. We stand up in church every Sunday and say, 'We believe in God the Father Almighty, and in Jesus Christ, His Son.'"

John asks the searching question: "Do they *confess* Him? Do they live by Him? Have they committed themselves to His ways? If not, don't follow them."

"Every spirit that does not acknowledge ["confess," RSV] Jesus is not from God" (v. 3). Christianity is not a creed or a ceremony, but a life connected with Jesus, our living Christ.

E. Stanley Jones said it powerfully: "Christ . . . unites us; . . . doctrines . . . divide."[77] If we ask a group of Christians, "*What* do you believe?" we'll hear conflicting debates. No two people believe exactly alike. If we ask, "*Whom* do you trust?" we are drawn together in the person of Jesus Christ. Dr. Jones once said, "We must call men, not to loyalty to a belief, but loyalty to a Person . . . But we do not get Jesus from our beliefs; we get our beliefs from Jesus."[78]

A doctor lay dying. A Christian doctor sat beside him. Gently he urged the dying man to have faith in Jesus. Listening in amazement, the dying doctor suddenly understood. The light dawned. He said joyfully, "All my life I have been bothered about what to believe. Now I see it is whom to trust!"

"Every spirit who is confessing Jesus as Christ come in the flesh is of God." That means accepting and acting upon two facts.

First, *Jesus is the Christ, God's Messiah.* To deny that truth is to deny Jesus as the One for whom all history was a preparation. It is to deny that Jesus is the Fulfillment of God's promises. It is to deny that Jesus came to accept a cross and to found a kingdom. Jesus is God's Anointed One—past, present, and future.

Second, *Jesus came in human flesh.* Bible students use the word *incarnation.* Grocery shoppers have seen cans labeled "Chili con carne." It means "chili with meat or flesh." The word *incarnation* describes God coming in flesh—Jesus Christ is God in flesh—humanity. Gnostics, whom John was combating, taught that the physical body was inherently evil. Therefore, either Jesus was not God because God could not put on evil flesh, or Jesus was only a phantom or ghost—He only appeared to be in human form. Either one is the wrong Jesus. Don't compromise. The Bible test for recognizing the true teacher or true group is this: "Every spirit who is confessing Jesus as Christ come in the flesh is of God." To deny that truth makes nonsense out of Jesus as Savior. The great truth of the incarnate Christ is that we can have real communion with God here and now! Jesus is not simply man's view of God, but God's view of himself. Jesus is God come to us.

Beware of anyone who tries to make Jesus into something else. Cerinthus, chief spokesman for the Gnostics, said that Christ came *into* the flesh. According to Cerinthus, Christ entered into the flesh of the man, Jesus, at His baptism and left the man, Jesus, before His crucifixion. That kind of Christ can save no one.

A New England preacher said, "Beware of Bible commentators who are unwilling to take God's words just as they stand." In the Garden of Eden, the devil proposed only a slight change in God's word to Adam and Eve. He simply inserted the word "not" into God's word, so that it became: "You will not die" (Gen. 3:4, RSV). Eve accepted that first amendment, and a world was lost!

In every generation people insist, "God didn't really mean what He said." And then they begin to interpret in rebellion to God's Word. There are even theological professors who twist the Word of God. In 1965 I wished to enter a doctoral program at a noted university's seminary. Upon examination, I found not one professor who believed "Jesus as Christ come in the flesh"!

John warns: "Every spirit that does not acknowledge Jesus is not from God. This is the spirit of the antichrist, which you have heard is coming and even now is already in the world" (v. 3). Almost every deviant form of Christianity distorts the person of Jesus. Jesus was either God in flesh, or He is not worth considering. C. S. Lewis put it clearly:

> I am trying to prevent anyone from saying the really silly thing that people often say about Him: "I'm ready to accept Jesus as a great moral teacher, but I don't accept His claim to be God." That's the one thing we mustn't say. A man who was merely a man and said the sort of things Jesus said wouldn't be a great moral teacher. He'd either be a lunatic—on a level with the man who says he's a poached egg—or else he'd be the Devil of Hell. You must make your choice. Either this man was, and is, the Son of God, or else a madman or something worse. You can shut Him up for a fool, you can spit at Him and kill Him as a demon; or you can fall at His feet and call Him Lord and God. But don't let us come with any patronizing nonsense about Him being a great human teacher. He hasn't left that open to us. He didn't intend to.[79]

John calls those who refuse Jesus as Christ come in the flesh "antichrist." The prefix *anti* can mean "against" or "instead of." Many false teachers and groups do not openly oppose Jesus but offer substitutes—a substitute Christ, a substitute salvation, or even a substitute Bible. They offer you something *instead of* the real Word of God and real eternal life. But if they deny Jesus Christ, they are not of God, no matter what they do or say. John the Baptist proclaimed, "Whoever believes in the Son has eternal life, but whoever rejects the Son will not see life, for God's wrath remains on him" (John 3:36). The crucial question is this: "What do you think of Jesus?" You answer for life or death!

III. DON'T BE AFRAID: CHRIST IN YOU GIVES VICTORY OVER THE WORLD AROUND YOU

"You, dear children"—you with childlike trust who believe God's Word—"are from God and have overcome them" (v. 4). In the Greek text, the word "overcome" is in the perfect tense, meaning a past completed victory with a continuing result. Jesus won the victory at the Cross, and He abides within us right now, making us strong and victorious.

Now comes one of John's most exciting statements: "The one who is in you is greater than the one who is in the world" (v. 4). John focuses on the continuing ministry of God's Spirit. These Christians had not delivered themselves from false teachers, but the One who dwelt within them had kept them straight. Satan may be powerful and deceptive, but "greater is he that is in you, than he that is in the world" (KJV). We may be ordinary people, but we have an extraordinary Christ within. The Holy Spirit is a foolproof sin-alarm system. We can have complete overwhelming victory over Satan's power and deceptions. Satan is mighty, but Jesus is Almighty! With Jesus we fight a defeated foe.

A Christian teacher was greatly respected by his students. In times of strain and stress, he evidenced poise and peace. One day a student asked, "Sir, what's your secret? Things that would shake us don't seem to rattle you. Don't testings and temptations bother you? Aren't you ever tempted to do wrong?"

The teacher responded, "I know something of what you speak. Enticements to do wrong come to me too. But when these temptations knock at the door of my heart, I say to the tempter, 'This place is occupied.'"

"Greater is he that is in you, than he that is in the world." Those words seem to recall Elisha's statement to his young servant. The armies of the enemy had moved in during the night and camped around the city where Elisha and his servant slept. When the servant shook sleep from his eyes in the morning, he was startled by the army with horses and chariots. Elisha comforted him. "Don't be afraid . . . Those who are with us are more than those who are with them." Then Elisha prayed, "O Lord, open his eyes so he may see." The Bible says, "Then the Lord opened the servant's eyes, and he looked and saw the hills full of horses and chariots of fire all around Elisha" (2 Kings 6:16-17).

As Christians we have within us One with more power and more authority than all the legions of darkness and error: "Greater is he that is in you, than he that is in the world."

That's reason to rejoice!

14

Love—Pass It On

▽

1 JOHN 4:7-12

△

*I*N 1796 HARMAN Blennerhassett migrated to America from Ireland. This rich revolutionary character got involved with Aaron Burr and financed his schemes for an empire. He lost it all. Burr's biographer said of Harman: "Like many revolutionaries, he liked the common people best in absentia."

In contrast, the dominant theme of the New Testament is love—genuine love. For the third time, the apostle John deals with the subject of love. No other New Testament book concentrates on love as does 1 John. The apostle was writing to believers who had resisted the Gnostics' false teachings. They had stood by the truth and kept their moral lives pure. However, John wonders, "Do you love one another?" Belief in Jesus and obedience to God's commands cannot be separated from loving one another.

Jerome, an early Christian, told of John living in Ephesus in his old age. His disciples had to carry him into the church. With no strength left for preaching, the aged apostle John would simply say, "Little children, love one another." Each time he gave the same instruction: "Little children, love one another."

Weary of the repeated refrain, the brothers asked, "Master, why do you always say this?"

His ancient voice spoke clearly, "Because it is the

Lord's command. If that alone is done, it will be sufficient!"

Once we have settled the question of "becoming" Christians, the big question is, "Are we willing to *be* Christians?" Then, "Love one another." Three times in six verses John urges us, "Love one another." And each time he tells us an important fact about God. To each of these three facts John links one of the Persons of the Trinity. The first is given in the context of God the Father (vv. 7-8); the second in the context of God the Son (vv. 9-11); and the third in the context of God the Holy Spirit (v. 12). In other words, "Love one another" because God the Father is love, God the Son is love, and God the Holy Spirit is love.

I. GOD'S LOVE IS PERSONIFIED IN HIMSELF, SO LOVE ONE ANOTHER

"Dear friends, let us love one another, for love comes from God. Everyone who loves has been born of God and knows God. Whoever does not love does not know God, because God is love" (vv. 7-8).

God is the Source of love: "for love comes from God" *(ek tou theou)* (v. 7). Love has its origins in God. Actually John speaks of "the love"—with a definite article. He refers specifically to God's kind of self-giving love. Behind all that God does is this self-giving love. Even His condemnations spring from love. His love opposes anything that is hurtful and destructive to those whom He loves. On the human level, if you attack a child in his mother's presence, you'll see a love that gets inflamed at anything that threatens her loved one. God's love is like that.

Knowledge of God leads to loving one another: "Whoever does not love does not know God, because God is love" (v. 8). Only by knowing God do we learn to love.

Paradoxically, only by loving do we learn to know God. In the Bible, the word "know" reaches deeper than intellectual understanding. In the Old Testament, the verb "to know" describes the intimate union of husband and wife (Gen. 4:1, KJV). To "know" God is to love Him in a deep, abiding relationship, to share His life and love.

Emphasizing love and neglecting truth produces a bland religion blind to the harsh realities of sin and evil. Emphasizing truth and neglecting love produces a cold, legalistic fundamentalism empty of life and joy and fellowship. Christian groups can cling to correct creeds and have impeccable moral conduct and yet have little love for one another. They don't "know" the right things about God. Knowing Bible facts alone doesn't take the place of love. "In fact," says Warren Wiersbe, "it can be a dangerous substitute if we are not careful."

God's nature is love: "God is love" (v. 8). This is John's profoundest announcement about God. He does not suggest "love is God." Two people may think they love each other, but it does not mean their love is holy and good. "Love" is not the standard; "God" is the standard of righteousness. "Love does not define God; God defines love." Wiersbe added, "All that God *does* expresses all that God *is*."[80] Love tests our relationship to God because "God is love." "Whoever does not love does not know God." His love is not past history; it is present reality—"God *is* love."

We have been made in the image and likeness of God. Since God is love, we too must love. That's why one's actions and responses tell the true story.

We need to learn to love one another *here* if we expect to love one another over *there*! Nobody knows what you mean by saying, "God is love," unless you live it *here*.

Love must communicate in words and deeds. How did God communicate His love?

II. GOD'S LOVE WAS PROVED IN HIS SON, SO LOVE ONE ANOTHER

"This is how God showed his love among us: He sent his one and only Son into the world that we might live through him. This is love: not that we loved God, but that he loved us and sent his Son as an atoning sacrifice for our sins. Dear friends, since God so loved us, we also ought to love one another" (vv. 9-11).

God's love could not remain in abstract form. He had to express it in His actions. God imprinted His love on human history by His "one and only Son." When John says, "God *showed* his love," he means God "came out into the open" and "made His love public." What happened to Jesus was no accident; it was an appointment.

First, God gave *His Son*. His love holds nothing back. God gave the best He had. Paul marveled: "He who did not spare his own Son, but gave him up for us all—how will he not also, along with him, graciously give us all things?" (Rom. 8:32). With Paul we rejoice, "Thanks be to God for his indescribable gift!" (2 Cor. 9:15).

Second, God gave His Son *to die*. Jesus didn't come just to teach us about himself. He didn't come simply to be an example for us. The Lord came to die, to be executed like a criminal. He came to die "that we might live through him" (v. 9).

Paul was overwhelmed by the fact that nothing "in all creation, will be able to separate us from the love of God that is in Christ Jesus our Lord" (Rom. 8:39). William Barclay says, "The Cross is the proof that there is no length to which the love of God will refuse to go in order to win men's hearts . . . the Cross is the final proof of the love of God."

At the Cross, God took our punishment on himself.

"He bore the sin of many" (Isa. 53:12). A young convert to Christianity saw two groups of Malkanas, Muslims of India, fighting with iron-tipped bamboo poles. He ran between them and took the blows on his own head. Blood flowed down and stained his white clothes. Both sides stopped fighting. Some ran for a doctor; others took him into their home. From that moment a reconciliation took place. He commented, "If a few drops of blood of a sinful man can reconcile a whole village, how much more can the blood of God's Son reconcile the world."

Third, God gave His Son to die *for sinners.* His love is totally undeserved. "But God demonstrates his own love for us in this: While we were still sinners, Christ died for us" (Rom. 5:8). God sent Jesus to be our Atoning Sacrifice. We can't be saved by perfect obedience because we can't give it. We can't be saved by imperfect obedience because God can't accept it. The only solution is the cross of Christ. Jesus can restore our lost relationship with God. He pardons our sins at His own cost. The Bible says, "He appeared so that he might take away our sins" (1 John 3:5). Charles Spurgeon said his theology could be condensed into four words: "Jesus died for me."

On the Scottish seacoast, an estuary only two miles wide was so long it took a lengthy journey by land to get to the other side. The estuary divided the people until it was spanned by the great Firth Bridge, which united them from both shores.

Until Jesus came, a great gulf was fixed between us and God. Because God gave His Son to die for us, "now in Christ Jesus you who once were far away have been brought near through the blood of Christ" (Eph. 2:13).

"This is love: not that we loved God, but that he loved us" (v. 10). God did not withhold His love until we reached out for Him. He came down to us. A little chorus says:

I love Him; I love Him
Because He first loved me,
And purchased my salvation
On Calv'ry's tree.

A father asked his two children why they loved him. Immediately they listed all the things normal parents provide for their children. "You buy our food, clothes, and things we want. You buy us candy and toys—"

Finally he asked: "Do you know why I love you so much?" The children were silent. He said, "I love you so much because you are my children. I love you and I can't help it."

"Dear friends, since God so loved us, we also ought to love one another" (v. 11). People give lame excuses: "I just can't love that person. You don't understand what he is like. If you had to live with him, you couldn't love him either."

John answers, "Since God so loved us, we also ought to love one another." You not only *can* love them, you "ought" to love them—you owe it to them! The Greek grammar of the text says you have a continuing obligation to be loving to one another. Love is your only obligation!

III. GOD'S LOVE IS PERFECTED IN HIS PEOPLE, SO LOVE ONE ANOTHER

"No one has ever seen God; but if we love one another, God lives in us and his love is made complete in us" (v. 12).

John says, "No one has ever seen God." How is a person to know Him?

John's breathtaking statement is that although God cannot be seen in himself, He can be seen in those who "love one another." "If we love one another, God lives in us." We are to love another person because he really is somebody. God wants to have a relationship with him. Each person brims with every longing, heartache, hope, dream, and frustration common to you and me. Love reaches out as an equal: "What can I do to help?"

Real love keeps on through life's ups and downs. The Greek grammar suggests, "If we *keep on* loving one another." If we keep on loving, we experience the presence of God in our hearts and lives.

"And his love is made complete in us." That sounds fantastic—God's love is not completed in angels, but in men and women who once lived in rebellion but have been saved by grace. God's love finds completion only when it is reproduced in us. Until we "love one another," God's love has not yet reached His goal. We have short-circuited His expression of love. As we love, His love is finally complete. We aren't spectators. We are participants in the drama of God's love.

Warren Wiersbe illustrated:

> In order to save money, a college drama class purchased only a few scripts of a play and cut them up into separate parts. The director gave each player his individual part in order and then started to rehearse the play. But nothing went right. After an hour of missed cues and mangled sequences, the cast gave up.
>
> At that point, the director sat the actors all on the stage and said: "Look, I'm going to read the entire play to you, so don't any of you say a word." He read the entire script aloud, and when he was finished, one of the actors said:
>
> "So that's what it was all about!"
>
> And when they understood the entire story, they were able to fit their parts together and have a successful rehearsal.[81]

"If we love one another, God lives in us and his love is made complete in us." When you read that, you feel like saying, "So that's what it's all about!" We discover what

God has in mind. His love, demonstrated in Jesus, is made complete in His people as they "love one another."

It's not our love being perfected, but God's love being perfected in us. We begin to love with a love not our own. We begin to love even impossible people. As we love, God is loving through us. In the context of loving our enemies, Jesus said, "Be perfect, therefore, as your heavenly Father is perfect" (Matt. 5:48). He perfects His love in us as we respond in love.

Ray Stedman pointed out, "As long as we are nice only to our friends or to those who are nice to us, no one has any idea that God is around. But when we start being nice to those who are nasty to us, when we start returning good for evil, when we start being patient . . . thoughtful, and considerate of those who are stubborn . . . and selfish and say difficult things to us, the people get the sense that God is somewhere around, close at hand, that He is in the situation. Then God's dwelling in us becomes visible to them."[82]

Someone said, "A saint is a man in whom Christ lives again." Dr. Leslie Weatherhead noted, "Love, even the love of God, is only mediated through persons."

A Salvation Army worker found a derelict woman alone on the street and invited her to come into the chapel for help. The woman stubbornly refused to move. The worker assured her: "We love you and want to help you. God loves you. Jesus died for you." However, the woman wouldn't budge.

Then, spontaneously, the Army lassie leaned over and kissed the woman on the cheek. The woman began to sob and was led like a child into the chapel. Soon she accepted Jesus Christ as Savior.

Later, she said, "You *told* me that God loves me, but it wasn't till you *showed* me that God loves me that I wanted to be saved."[83]

No one has seen God. If God's people love one another, we reveal our family likeness to a world in need. As we love, God's love accomplishes its full purpose.

Dana Walling, then a youth pastor, joined the excitement at a Special Olympics track meet. The athletes compete against their own physical handicaps as much as against each other. The explosion of the starter's pistol launched the runners into the 440-yard race. There were only two runners. At the first turn, Joey was ahead by 10 yards. The coach shouted to his athlete: "Go, Joey! You're winning, Joey! Keep it up! Attaboy, Joey!"

With determination both boys struggled to keep up the garbled communication between mind and limb. Rounding the last turn, Joey was heading into the final stretch. The coach shouted, "Come on, Joey! You're killing him, Joey!"

Suddenly Joey stopped in his tracks. The coach screamed, "Joey! What are you doing? Keep going! Don't you want to win?"

Only 25 yards from the finish line, Joey turned around and grinned at his competitor chugging along like the little train that could. Joey started yelling and waving, "Come on! You can do it! Attaboy!" The other boy's face broke into a huge smile—and he ran a little faster.

As the gap narrowed between them, Joey reached out his hand. Silence hung over the track momentarily as Joey and his friend trotted to the finish line hand in hand.

In the early part of the race, seeing Joey struggle, Dana Walling said inwardly, "O God, thank You that I am not like him!"

As Joey crossed the finish line, Dana's prayer changed: "O God, please help me to be more like him!"

"If we love one another . . . his love is made complete in us."

15

Nobody's Perfect—in Man's Opinion!

▽

1 JOHN 4:13-21

△

*W*HEN IT WAS to their advantage, my daughters used to remind me, "Dad, nobody's perfect!" I can't imagine any parent claiming to be perfect.

People view perfection with suspicion. Strangely, we expect perfection out of pilots and airplanes—or we wouldn't consider flying. But when it comes to living, we are suspicious of those who appear perfect. Perfection, real or imagined, creates distance; weakness unites. We don't feel close to successful people unless we know they have struggled. I found that "the only good thing about being imperfect is the joy it brings to others."

Ever since the Bible came out in English, we have had trouble over 1 John 4 with its references to "perfect love." Even Jesus' words have been puzzling: "Be perfect, therefore, as your heavenly Father is perfect" (Matt. 5:48). The English word "perfect," in popular perception, carries the idea of "without defect; faultless; having no mistake, error, flaw." Who but Jesus could live up to that?

The New Testament Greek word for "perfect" carries the idea of completeness, full-grown, adult, fulfillment. Its basic concept is fulfillment of created purpose. The Greek word suggests "to make complete" or "to finish." Jesus said, "My food is to do the will of him who sent me and *to finish* his work" (John 4:34). In Jesus' Pastoral Prayer, He said, "I have brought you glory on earth *by completing* the work you gave me to do" (John 17:4, all italics added).

Something is perfect—in the biblical sense—when it fulfills the purpose for which it was designed. My new book does not fulfill its purpose if you use it only for a doorstop or as a hot pad for your coffeepot. It is only a perfect book if you read it and understand. That's the purpose for which it was intended.

For emphasis, John repeats his most important definition: "God is love" (v. 16). E. Stanley Jones wrote, "When that phrase was about to be written, all heaven bent over in anticipation to see whether John would really write it, for it had never been said before in human history. When John did write it, heaven broke out in applause: 'They've got it. They have really seen it—God is love!'"[84]

In the remainder of 1 John 4, the apostle speaks of "perfect love," love that has fulfilled God's purpose. The term "perfect love" appears nowhere else in the Bible. In the Greek text it is mentioned here four times: once each in verses 12 and 17 and twice in 18. Three times the Greek perfect tense is employed, suggesting that "we are upheld and kept in this experience." Three times the Greek passive voice is used, which means that "perfect love is something that is happening to us. It is not something we do, but what God does, and so He gets the credit, not us."[85]

"Perfect love" is basic to the Bible doctrine of holiness. Holiness that doesn't touch our hearts with love made complete is hollow and harsh. We are not made perfect in love apart from God; rather, His love is made perfect or complete in us.

A word of caution: John is speaking of perfection in

love, not in performance. When a father came home after a long absence, his little boy was so happy that he wanted to show his love for his father. He asked, "Daddy, can't I do something for you?"

His father asked for a glass of water. The excited little fellow rushed to the kitchen, poured some water in a used glass, spilled some on the table, and hurried back, two little dirty fingers grasping the glass on the inside. As the father took the gift of love, he saw two little muddy streams trickling down the inside of the used glass. That father drank every drop without blinking an eye.

That little boy's love was perfect, but his performance was imperfect. His father basked in the love and never mentioned the imperfections. Dr. Purkiser noted, "Biblical perfection is not faultlessness but blamelessness. It is perfection of heart, not of 'head' or 'hand.' It relates to intention, not intelligence; to love, not life; to purity, not performance. It has to do with deliverance from sin, not from ignorance, mistakes, infirmities, temptation, or the constant necessity for watchfulness and prayer."[86]

A second word of caution: John is speaking of a "perfect love" that demands growth and maturity. "Oswald Chambers . . . often said, God can give us pure hearts in an instant, but He cannot quickly give us Christian character."[87] All Christians have room for growth in a love for others.

A little child learning to walk staggers with faltering steps to his mother across the room. Each time he progresses a little farther while the parents exclaim, "Our baby is walking!" That child is walking perfectly for a child of that age—but two more years will bring a lot of improvement.

Perfect love implies growth and maturity, otherwise it would be blemished and imperfect. Growth and maturity are signs of life.

The love God intends will grow. The clerk asked the elderly man if he needed help at the greeting card counter. He responded, "It's our 40th wedding anniversary. Forty years ago I wouldn't have had trouble picking out a card for her. I thought I knew what love was then. But after 40 years, we love each other so much more that I can't find a card that says what I want to say!"

That should be our growing experience with God's love and our growing expression of love to others. What does perfect love do in the believer's life? John gives three answers.

I. PERFECT LOVE GIVES CONFIDENCE

Perfect love prepares us for God's future: "Love is *made complete* among us so that we will have confidence on the day of judgment, because in this world we are like him" (v. 17). We can face the coming Day of Judgment without pretending. We don't have to impress anyone. Wiersbe noted, "Pretending is one of the favorite activities of little children, but it is certainly not a mark of maturity in adults." Perfect love gives us confidence before the Judge of all. The Day of Judgment is coming on God's scheduled timetable, and we can face it with assurance through God's indwelling love.

The subject of God's judgment is not popular today. People don't like to face the idea of having to account to Him for their actions. They dismiss the idea of judgment, but they cannot escape the fact of judgment. The person in whom God's love is made complete doesn't have to face condemnation. We don't fear the One who loves us. In Him we stand confident. The same Jesus we met as Redeemer shall sit as Judge in that day—and we are on His team. Since our sins were washed away forever by Jesus' full atonement, we can have confidence in God's love even at the Day of Judgment. Why should we be confident? Because our case is not coming up.

Jesus said, "Whoever hears my word and believes him who sent me has eternal life and will not be condemned; he has crossed over from death to life" (John 5:24).

If, for any reason, you are anxious and concerned about the Day of Judgment, you can settle that question today and settle it forever!

II. PERFECT LOVE GIVES COURAGE

Perfect love drives out fear: "There is no fear in love. But perfect love drives out fear, because fear has to do with punishment. The one who fears is not made perfect in love" (v. 18).

John introduces a new word into his written sermon: "fear." Is it possible that believers may live in fear? One writer said, "If people are afraid, it is because of something in the past that haunts them, or something in the present that upsets them, or something in the future that they feel threatens them. Or . . . a combination of all three."[88] Some Christian groups encourage fear in their members as a way to manipulate them—but that's not the way of "perfect love."

Fear goes under the aliases of anxiety, worry, restlessness, boredom, and resentment. One man only accepts second-rate jobs out of "fear of failure." He takes only the jobs that don't tax his skills. He refuses first-rate assignments. He calls it "humility," but it is fear.

Loveless Christianity operates in fear. Behind fear is the pain of not feeling loved. Nothing cures fear like the deep assurance that we are loved. When love comes, fear goes. Immature Christians vacillate between fear and love;

Spirit-filled Christians rest in God's abiding love. "There is no fear in love."

Announcing the coming birth of Jesus, the angel said to Joseph, "Do not be afraid" (Matt. 1:20). Jesus' first words after His resurrection were "Do not be afraid" (28:10). His mission is to release people from fear. God's love removes guilt; therefore, "perfect love drives out fear, because fear has to do with punishment." Fear of punishment is gone when love is made complete in us.

Earl Lee, during his son's captivity in the Iranian hostage crisis, was learning the deep meaning of loving one's enemies. A newsman asked him, "What would you do if you met Khomeini?"

Lee replied sincerely, "I would say, 'I love you.'" A quotation from his reading had given inspiration: "Love is the only emotion that is not natural, the only one that has to be learned, and the only one that matters." God's perfect love dwelling in us gives us courage for all of life. "For you did not receive a spirit that makes you a slave again to fear, but you received the Spirit of sonship" (Rom. 8:15).

III. PERFECT LOVE GIVES CERTAINTY

Perfect love expressed to others proves our claim to love God: "We love because he first loved us. If anyone says, 'I love God,' yet hates his brother, he is a liar. For anyone who does not love his brother, whom he has seen, cannot love God, whom he has not seen. And he has given us this command: Whoever loves God must also love his brother" (vv. 19-21).

John insists on testing a person's fellowship with God by his love for his brothers. "We love because he first loved us." Our love is a response to His love. Here's the basis for all our dealings with other people. A child is a healthy child, not when he has no faults or defects, but when he knows the security of being loved by his father and mother. In the same way, we are most healthy when we realize we are surrounded by our Heavenly Father's love.

Love for God and hatred toward another person are incompatible: "If anyone says, 'I love God,' yet hates his brother, he is a liar."

"For anyone who does not love his brother, whom he has seen, cannot love God, whom he has not seen." The apostle John argues that it's easier to love a visible brother than an invisible God! Nobody has seen God, but His character has been revealed in Jesus, and His love is being made complete in us. Here's the test of "perfect love": is His love touching others through me?

Someone asked George Whitefield, "Is that man over there a Christian?"

Whitefield replied, "I don't know. I haven't talked to his wife."

Perfect love is proved by our love for our brothers and sisters—and wives. It's more than talk; it is primarily a walk.

Moishe Rosen, president of Jews for Jesus, called on a Jewish Christian girl who felt that she no longer wanted to come to church. She was adamant; under no circumstances did she want to attend that church—or any other. Having found the Lord, she had joined the church, had sung in the choir, had volunteered as a typist, and had given public testimony of her faith. Disowned by her family because of her faith in Jesus, she felt the church was now her family.

Suddenly faced with surgery, two weeks of hospitalization, and confinement to home for several weeks, she asked for prayer and admitted her need for help. The pastor said publicly, "Don't worry. We'll take care of whatever you need. Just give us a call." With that assurance, she went into the hospital.

No one visited from the church. When it was time to come home from the hospital, she telephoned her church for help, but the church secretary explained that they didn't do things like that. The pastor had gone home to his unlisted number. She went home in a taxi—and the unknown taxidriver helped her upstairs. With no food in the house, she called her church family again for help—but nothing. Her hopes were dashed. She had been loved in word but not in deed.

As representatives of Jesus, we must mean what we say. "Love" is a four-letter word that becomes obscene when it carries no real meaning. The word itself can become a prostitute. Jesus didn't go about simply telling people that He loved them; He showed them.

"And he has given us this command: Whoever loves God must also love his brother." We must show people that we love them because God loves us. Perfect love is love made visible in compassionate words and deeds.

At Pasadena College, a dozen people took a summer school course in "Group and Interpersonal Relations." To close the class, they decided to do something together. They had gotten to know each other and had shared their personal lives with each other. They decided to get together and hike to Hennigar Flats—about three miles up the side of the mountain behind the campus, a steep hour-and-a-half walk.

Reuben Welch tells us graphically:

> So they set the day and made the sandwiches and made the chocolate and brought the cold drinks and the back packs and they got all gathered up for the safari and they started up the mountain—together.

> But it wasn't long until the strong, stalwart ones were up in front and the other ones were back in the middle and way back at the end of the line was a girl named Jane—who was . . . out of shape.

At the front was Don—a big, strong, former paratrooper. He and some others—the strong ones—were up in front and the weak ones were back in the back and way in the back was Jane. And Don said . . . he looked back a couple of switchbacks and saw Jane and the Lord told him that he had just better go back and walk with her. That's kind of hard on him because he has a need to be first. But he went down and started walking with Jane and the people in the level above called down, "Come on up. It's great up here."

And Jane yelled, "I don't think I can make it."

And they hollered, "Yeah, you can. Try harder, come on up." And every time they called to her, down went her own sense of worth, down went her own sense of value—"I can't make it."

"Oh yeah, you can. Come on."

So the strong went on ahead and the weak hung behind and here was Jane and she never made it to the top.

Now, look what you have. You have a group—we know each other, we like each other, we want to do this together, let's go to Hennigar Flats together. But before long, you have divided the strong and the weak, the haves and the have-nots, and the ables and the unables. So what started out as a group has now become a fragmented collection. And so the strong say, "You can do it."

And the weak say, "No, I can't."

And the strong say, "Try harder"—which is a big help. That's a big help. And she didn't make it.

Thankfully, that's not the last chapter. They must have learned their lessons because they decided that was no way to end the fellowship of that class and they got together and decided to do it again. But they made some new rules—it was everybody go or nobody go and they were all going together. So they set the day and made the sandwiches and made the chocolate and brought the cold drinks and the back packs and they got all gathered up for the safari, and they started up the mountain. It took them four hours to make it to the top, and the water was all gone and the cold drinks were all gone and the sandwiches were all gone and the chocolate was all gone and the back packs were empty, but they all made it, together.

. . . we have got to go together. Christian fellowship is no place for get in or get out—it's get in, get in . . . It is God's intention that we go together as a body.[89]

"Whoever loves God must also love his brother."
How many of you are planning to go to heaven?
Who are you taking along?

16

Ancient History or Current Events?

▽

1 JOHN 5:1-12

△

A CHURCH SIGN ON the corner asked, "Is your Christian experience ancient history or current events?"

In his concluding chapter, the apostle John is concerned about up-to-date relationships with God and the brothers in Christ. The Bible tells us what Jesus did long ago, but it's important to know how you and Jesus are getting along today.

A missionary on furlough was dictating some letters to a public stenographer. In the midst of her dictation, the stenographer suddenly asked, "Who is Jesus?"

The missionary's references to Jesus had impressed the woman—so intimate, so natural, so current.

The missionary stopped her work. For several minutes she told of Jesus, who was real and dear to her. She spoke, not of a dead Jesus, but of a living Lord. The stenographer listened with astonishment. When the missionary concluded, the young lady said, "I never knew that Jesus was anything except a good man who lived 2,000 years ago."

Is your Christian experience ancient history or current events? Jesus desires to be your living Contemporary!

John introduces his fifth theme. He has written of fellowship, truth, righteousness, and love. Now he speaks of assurance—an ongoing confidence in Jesus Christ. John discusses our present belief in Jesus from three perspectives.

I. OUR OBEDIENCE VERIFIES OUR PRESENT BELIEF IN JESUS

John begins, "Everyone who believes that Jesus is the Christ is born of God" (v. 1). "Belief" is more than mental assent. "Belief" is a life-style. In fact, the word "belief" means literally "by life." Your belief is your life. Your life is your belief. Your deed is your creed. The old Anglo-Saxon word "belief" means "what you live by." People's actions are the best interpretations of their thoughts.

"Everyone who loves the father loves his child as well. This is how we know that we love the children of God: by loving God and carrying out his commands" (vv. 1-2). Christians don't *have to* love each other; they *want to* love each other because they are one family. Love seeks to serve. Are you seeking to serve God's family or are you one of those who love to be served? People who are always wanting others to do for them are never a happy group. They are always feeling hurt and slighted. But those merry souls whose love is "current events" are delightfully different.

"This is love for God: to obey his commands" (v. 3). Our obedience to God verifies our up-to-date love for Him. The Greek word for "to obey" means "to guard" or "to keep watch over." The only part of the Bible you really believe is the part you obey! Our love for Him is not an emotion, but a guiding principle for life. Dwight L. Moody said, "Every Bible should be bound in shoe leather." Empty words do not express our love for God, but willing obedience does. We should not read the Bible as a textbook, but as a love letter.

Warren Wiersbe pointed out:

> The longest chapter in the Bible is Psalm 119, and its theme is the Word of God. Every verse but two mentions the Word of God in one form or another, as law, precepts, commandments, etc. But the interesting thing is that the Psalmist *loves* the Word of God and enjoys telling us about it! "O how love I thy law!" (Ps. 119:97, KJV).
>
> Imagine turning *statutes* into *songs*. Suppose the local symphony presented an evening of the traffic code set to music! Most of us do not consider laws a source of joyful song, but this is the way the Psalmist looked at God's law. Because he loved the Lord, he loved His law.[90]

If you profess to be a Christian, but you don't delight in God's will, you are grieving the Holy Spirit. Something in your life is dishonoring God. That's why the joy is gone. You need to find out what in your life is contrary to His Word. Bob Pierce, founder of World Vision, prayed, "O God, we ask not that You bless what we do, but that we do what You bless!"

That puts our obedience in the "current events" bracket.

John adds, "And his commands are not burdensome" (v. 3). Jesus himself said, "Come to me, all you who are weary and burdened, and I will give you rest. Take my yoke upon you and learn from me . . . For my yoke is easy and my burden is light" (Matt. 11:28-30). Because we love Him, we wish to serve and please Him. Love lightens burdens. In his pursuit for the woman he loved, "Jacob served seven years to get Rachel, but they seemed like only a few days to him because of his love for her" (Gen. 29:20).

With a note of triumph, John writes, "Everyone born of God has overcome the world. This is the victory that has overcome the world, even our faith. Who is it that overcomes the world? Only he who believes that Jesus is the Son of God" (vv. 4-5).

Since we have been born of God, we are overcomers! The words for "overcome," *nikaō,* and "victory," *nikē,* have the same Greek root. The Greek goddess of victory was Nike. It's also the source of the name Nicholas, which means "conqueror of the people." It suggests "to conquer in battle, to prevail, to vanquish." This conquering word appears 31 times in the New Testament, including seven times in John's Book of the Revelation. Paul's most dynamic use of the word is Rom. 12:21—"Do not be overcome by evil, but overcome evil with good." No doubt John learned it from Jesus, who said before going to Gethsemane for the last time, "Take heart! I have overcome the world" (John 16:33).

"Overcome" is in the present tense, signifying that we have a continuous victory in Jesus as we keep on believing and obeying Him. Faith is God's key to victory. The people of faith in Hebrews 11 won their victories by faith. They took God at His word and acted on it. He honored their faith by giving them victory.

Since "overcoming" and "believing" are in the present tense, John is not talking about the faith you exercised many years ago when you became a Christian. He refers to your habitual, ongoing, active trust in Christ today. "Who is it that overcomes [literally, "the one who keeps on conquering"] the world? Only he who believes that Jesus is the Son of God" (v. 5).

A preacher told this beautiful story:

A Civil War veteran used to wander from place to place, begging a bed and bite to eat and always talking about his friend, "Mr. Lincoln." Because of his injuries, he was unable to hold a stable job. But as long as he could keep going, he would chat about his beloved President.

"You say you knew Mr. Lincoln," a skeptical bystander retorted one day. "I'm not so sure you did. Prove it!"

The old man replied, "Why, sure, I can prove it. In fact,

I have a piece of paper here that Mr. Lincoln himself signed and gave to me."

From his old wallet, the man took out a much-folded piece of paper and showed it to the man. "I'm not much for reading," he apologized, "but I know that's Mr. Lincoln's signature."

"Man, do you know what you have here?" one of the spectators asked. "You have a generous Federal pension authorized by President Lincoln. You don't have to walk around like a poor beggar! Mr. Lincoln has made you rich!"

To paraphrase what John wrote: "You Christians do not have to walk around defeated, because Jesus Christ has made you victors! He has defeated every enemy and you share His victory. Now, *by faith,* claim His victory."[91]

All that God has promised is available to the one who believes.

II. GOD'S WITNESS AFFIRMS OUR PRESENT BELIEF IN JESUS

"This is the one who came by water and blood—Jesus Christ. He did not come by water only, but by water and blood. And it is the Spirit who testifies, because the Spirit is the truth. For there are three that testify: the Spirit, the water and the blood; and the three are in agreement" (vv. 6-8).

John is saying that our belief in Jesus is founded upon reliable witnesses. According to Old Testament law, "One witness is not enough . . . A matter must be established by the testimony of two or three witnesses" (Deut. 19:15).

Marshaling three foundational witnesses for our faith in Jesus, John refers to them as "the water," "the blood," and "the Spirit." "The water" symbolizes Jesus' baptism. In that act of baptism, He fulfilled the righteousness of the law. At the same moment He was set apart by the Spirit, who descended like a dove upon Him, anointing Him as Messiah.

The second witness is "the blood." This refers to Jesus' death on the Cross in our behalf. Our atonement and conciliation with God are wrapped up in Jesus' substitutionary death. Paul exclaimed, "Christ died for our sins" (1 Cor. 15:3).

The third witness is "the Spirit." The witness of the Spirit verifies Jesus as God's Son. When our sins have been forgiven, the Spirit of God witnesses to our spirits by lifting the sense of guilt and giving the peace of God.

The director of a mental hospital in London told Billy Graham, "Half of our patients could be immediately dismissed if they could obtain somehow the assurance of forgiveness." The Bible says, "The Spirit himself testifies with our spirit that we are God's children" (Rom. 8:16).

As he lay dying, Samuel Wesley, vicar of Epworth, said to his son John, "The inward witness, son, the inward witness—*that* is the surest proof of Christianity!" The apostle John says, "Anyone who believes in the Son of God has this testimony in his heart" (v. 10).

John Wesley later described the witness of the Spirit as "an inward impression on the soul, whereby the Spirit of God immediately and directly bears witness to my spirit, that I am a child of God; that Christ has loved me, and given himself for me; that all my sins are blotted out, and I, even I, am reconciled to God."

Our present, up-to-date, and ongoing belief in Jesus is affirmed by God's witness. Our relationship with Him can be "current events."

III. ETERNAL LIFE CONFIRMS OUR PRESENT BELIEF IN JESUS

"And this is the testimony: God has given us eternal life, and this life is in his Son" (v. 11). The idea of "eternal life" is more than a life lasting forever. The human spirit lasts forever—the concept of "immortality." Everyone has immortal life—and that surprises many people.

Dr. Lloyd Ogilvie was called by the police to hurry to a young lady's home. When he arrived, the fireman had just smashed in a window and found the woman with her head in the oven, gasping. She cried, "Am I still alive? I wanted to stop living."

Dr. Ogilvie counseled, "You can end the life of your physical body, but you would spend eternity in the same spiritual condition in which you put your head in that oven!"

She, like others, assumed that physical death is the final liberation. There's immortal life after death. The only question is where, how, and with whom will we spend eternity? Immortality and eternal life are not the same things.

Eternal life is a quality of life—the life of God shared in His believers. John tells us three things about eternal life: it is undeserved; it is found only in Christ; and this gift is a present possession. We don't die before getting eternal life: "this life is in his Son." To accept Jesus into your heart and life is to possess eternal life.

The apostle puts it simply: "He who has the Son has life; he who does not have the Son of God does not have life" (v. 12). That's exactly what John concluded in his Gospel: "But these are written that you may believe that Jesus is the Christ, the Son of God, and that by believing you may have life in his name" (20:31). John didn't simply record "ancient history." He wrote to bring our relationship with God up to "current events." We can experience His life here and now. In the present tense, "Believe in the Lord Jesus, and you will be saved" (Acts 16:31).

The most important question is this: "Do you have the Son?" That question demands a decision. People don't ooze into fellowship with God. Each person must come to Jesus himself. "He who has the Son has life." If we meet and you forget me, you have lost nothing. But if you meet Jesus and forget Him, you have lost everything: "He who does not have the Son of God does not have life" (v. 12).

The 19-year-old paratrooper named Skip Jackson was called "the Punk." He served on active duty in Vietnam. Skip was born in New York City and grew up in a hostile environment filled with conflict and immorality. He learned to survive by being mean and tough. His mother was an alcoholic; his father, a drug addict. Lacking love, he learned to hate.

At 17, Skip entered the military and worked hard to get ahead—stepping on anyone in the way. At last he became a sergeant with the authority and personality to command.

In December of 1966, he found himself squad leader of a reconnaissance platoon in the delta region of Vietnam. During battle he smiled and laughed. When he killed his first Viet Cong, he spit on the body and walked away grinning.

Sergeant Jackson didn't like medics—they had something he couldn't understand: love and compassion for people. His platoon medic always smiled and talked about Jesus. The more he spoke, the more Skip hated him. The medic suffered as the target of Skip's abuse. One night Skip even put a bamboo viper in the medic's boots. But the medic's faith and joy in the Lord never wavered.

One morning the team went on a search-and-destroy mission. The sun was coming up over the trees. Birds were singing. In the distance, they could hear children laughing. Suddenly a blast of gunfire—and the quiet morning was ripped with pain and death.

Sergent Jackson fell to the ground—a wound in his

chest. He knew he was dying. As his eyes dimmed, his mind drifted back to the days when he laughed at God and the church. Was there something to it after all?

Quickly the medic stood over Skip, ripped off his shirt, and began applying first aid to the terrible wound. Since Skip had B-positive blood, he began setting up for a direct transfusion.

"Who's giving me blood, Doc?"

"I am."

"Why? Why should you give me blood and try to save me?"

Already inserting the plastic tube into the vein, the medic replied, "Because I love you—because you have an eternal spirit."

The life-giving blood flowed from the medic into the wounded sergeant. And the medic told Skip about Jesus— the One who died for those who hated Him: "While we were still sinners, Christ died for us" (Rom. 5:8). "The blood of Jesus, his Son, purifies us from all sin" (1 John 1:7). Skip got an object lesson in the power of Jesus' blood. The medic said, "Jesus, by giving His blood 2,000 years ago, gave a spiritual transfusion that crosses all time barriers. His blood still has the power to save."

The Punk cried, "I want to know your Jesus!"

Right then and there he found God's love and forgiveness. "He who has the Son has life!"

How about you? Have you personally experienced Jesus' power to save? Is your relationship to Him "ancient history" or "current events"?

17

God Keeps His Word

▽

1 JOHN 5:13-21

△

GOD ALWAYS KEEPS His Word. You can depend on Him.

Alfred P. Sloan, one of the creators and president of General Motors Corporation, was devastated when his wife of 50 years died. He called for the preaching pastor of Marble Collegiate Church, Dr. Norman Vincent Peale. Sloan said, "I want to ask you a question. I don't want any weasel answer or philosophical discussion. I want a straightforward 'yes' or 'no' answer. If you don't know the answer, say so. Will I meet my wife again?"

Dr. Peale, knowing about the Christian lady, said, "The answer is 'yes.'"

"How sure are you?"

"One hundred percent sure."

"Why are you so sure?"

"Because she loved Jesus. She was committed to Christ. She believed in the risen Lord and the Son of God. The Bible tells us that if we believe on Jesus, even though we die, yet shall we live. Where Jesus is, we will be also." Then Dr. Peale quoted 1 John 5:11-13: "God has given us eternal life, and this life is in his Son. He who has the Son has life . . . I write these things to you who believe in the name of the Son of God so that you may know that you have eternal life."

The businessman said, "I, too, believe. I do have the Son of God. I was weak and felt alone. I needed someone to talk to me like a man and a Christian." Putting his hand on the pastor's shoulder, he said, "I shall meet her in that 'land that is fairer than day.'" He found assurance in God's Word.[92]

Many Christians are discouraged because they don't feel sure that they are saved. Some Christians have difficulty believing that God's Word includes them—it's too good to be true, it seems. But we can know that we belong to God.

The word "know" is found 200 times in the Bible. The word "guess" is not found at all. Our trust in God's Word is based on facts—the fact of Jesus' ministry, the fact of His cross, the fact of His empty tomb, the fact of His resurrection established by eyewitnesses. We cannot believe anything into existence. Fact precedes faith.

Jesus' disciples testified about firsthand knowledge of facts: "We did not follow cleverly invented stories when we told you about the power and coming of our Lord Jesus Christ, but we were eyewitnesses of his majesty" (2 Pet. 1:16).

The apostle John concludes his written sermon with the note of assurance: "I write these things to you . . . so that you may know that you have eternal life" (v. 13). John has used the word "know" in his sermon more than 30 times. No Christian, when asked if he belongs to Jesus, needs to say, "I hope so" or "I think so."

A pastor asked a man, "Are you a Christian?"

The fellow replied, "No, but I wish I were."

The minister then quoted some verses from the Bible, but the man said bluntly, "The fact is, I cannot *feel* that I am saved."

The pastor asked, "Was it Noah's feelings that saved him, or was it Noah's ark?"

After thinking it over a moment, the man said, "It's all settled. I know I am saved!"

Assurance is not based on our feelings. Assurance is based on the character of God—One who keeps His Word. That's why in this closing section, John boldly uses the phrase "We know" four times. John knows that God keeps His Word.

I. GOD KEEPS HIS WORD ABOUT ANSWERING PRAYER

We turn to prayer when we don't know what else to do. John speaks of prayer with the ring of reality: "This is the confidence we have in approaching God: that if we ask anything according to his will, he hears us" (v. 14).

John doesn't use the word "pray." He emphasizes the common word in Jesus' teachings on prayer: "ask." Having grown up at Jesus' side, prayer to John was an intimate face-to-face conversation—not a formality.

Modern prayer life is similar to the two old-timers having a heated discussion. One did most of the talking. For several minutes the second man waited for an opening to present his side of the argument. Just when it appeared the first old-timer was about to run down and the second fellow could get in a few words, the talker summed up his arguement strongly, and then promptly turned off his hearing aid!

The apostle John makes an important distinction in the nature of prayer: "if we ask anything *according to his will.*" The "anything" is qualified by "according to his will." Some people have been misled by the idea that if they have enough faith, they will get whatever they ask. Faith is not the only qualification. The foundation of prayer is "according to his will." This is more than adding the postscript "if it be Your will" to our requests.

We must learn to ask for that which God wills to give. Answers to prayer are limited by His purposes. Prayer is not asking Him for whatever we want, but asking Him for whatever He wants.

The believer seeks and accepts God's will. He aligns himself with God's purposes. Every prayer should be a variation of the theme: "Thy will be done." God's will is revealed in His Word. Requests must be tailored to His known will. Wiersbe noted, "God has promised to supply our needs—not our greed!"

Test your requests by asking, "Could I stand before Jesus and unashamedly ask for this? Could I say to Jesus, 'Give me this for *Your* sake and in *Your* name'?"

Church prayer meetings sometimes become whining pleas of unbelief. With a begging tone of voice, the group attempts to persuade God to do something He is reluctant to do. But He is not like that! "If we ask . . . according to his will, he hears us. And if we know that he hears us—whatever we ask—*we know* that we have what we asked of him" (vv. 14-15, italics added). Here's the first "we know."

With assurance, John says in the present tense: "we *have* what we asked." Though we might not see the answer immediately, we are confident that God has heard and that His answer is on the way in His own time. The Bible says, "Now faith is being sure of what we hope for and certain of what we do not see" (Heb. 11:1). Paul exclaimed, "All the promises of God find their Yes in him" (2 Cor. 1:20, RSV). So, begin thanking Him for answered prayer!

At this point, John gives an illustration of a request definitely in God's will to answer—prayer for a brother who has stumbled morally or spiritually: "If anyone sees his brother commit a sin that does not lead to death, he should pray and God will give him life" (v. 16). Barclay said, "We naturally pray for those who are ill, and we should just as naturally pray for those who are straying away from God."[93]

Once in a while a preacher's illustration raises more

questions than it was intended to clarify. It seems John did that here: "I refer to those whose sin does not lead to death. There is a sin that leads to death. I am not saying that he should pray about that" (v. 16). Scholars debate, "What is this sin that leads to death?" Whatever it was, apparently John and his audience understood clearly, because John doesn't explain it. Since the key is lost, students of the Bible interpret according to their theological bias. This apparent riddle has stimulated so much curiosity about the sin unto death that it has overshadowed the duty of praying for an erring brother—the intent of John's illustration.

In case people think other sins don't matter much, John adds, "All wrongdoing is sin, and there is sin that does not lead to death" (v. 17). Our world makes a joke of sin, but any sin is serious with God. John's point is that, for example, you can always pray for "life" for people. That's why Jesus came: "I have come that they may have life, and have it to the full" (John 10:10). The prayer for a fallen brother would definitely be "according to his will."

Clement of Alexandria told a story about John of Ephesus—the author of 1 John—that took place in the closing years of the first century. During his travels as supervisor of the churches in what is modern-day Turkey, John committed a promising young Christian to a bishop's nurturing. The bishop discipled him faithfully until his baptism. After that, the bishop relaxed his efforts, thinking the young man had matured spiritually.

That young man became careless, fell into evil company, and went from bad to worse. He eventually led a gang of robbers.

Revisiting the area, John asked about the young man. When the bishop told him of the tragic fall, John called for his horse. He rode straight into the robbers' territory and was taken prisoner by them. John was taken to their chief, but the moment the young man recognized John, he ran away. In spite of his age, John chased him and caught up with him. After much pleading, John brought him back to the church.

Asking and acting on a fallen brother's behalf is certainly in accord with God's will.

II. GOD KEEPS HIS WORD ABOUT VICTORY OVER SIN

Here's the second "We know."

"We know that anyone born of God does not continue to sin; the one who was born of God keeps him safe, and the evil one cannot harm him" (v. 18).

The world of John's day was bogged down in moral defeat. It knew no escape. Seneca admitted, "Men hate their sins but cannot leave them." One fellow was described as "deadened by vice . . . who has no sense of sin, no knowledge of what he is losing, and is sunk so deep that he sends no bubble to the surface."

In contrast, John declares the Christian is freed from the power of sin. He comes to the place where he cannot continue to sin. The Bible says, "Everyone who confesses the name of the Lord must turn away from wickedness" (2 Tim. 2:19). Practicing sin proves one does not belong to God.

How does the believer keep from sinning? The Bible doesn't teach that a person can keep himself from sinning. A Christian must not depend on himself alone. Listen to the good news: "The one who was born of God [Jesus Christ] keeps him [the believer] safe." The one who keeps the believer is Jesus. John remembers Jesus praying on the eve of His crucifixion: "Holy Father . . . While I was with them, I protected them and kept them safe . . . My prayer is not that you take them out of the world but that you protect them from the evil one" (John 17:11-12, 15).

Though you may be weak, if you believe in Jesus, you are placed safely in Christ. What a wonderful place to be!

As the believer leans on Jesus, He keeps the believer safe, "and the evil one does not touch him" (RSV). The only other time this Greek word for "touch" appears in the New Testament is in John 20:17. On the Resurrection morning, Jesus appeared to Mary of Magdala and said, "Do not *hold* on to me" (italics added). It means "grasping hold of." Satan can't grasp hold of the born-again believer. Satan cannot "repossess" the Christian!

Stedman pointed out,

> The enemy can frighten us . . . He can harass us, he can threaten us, he can make us believe that we are in his power and that we have to do certain things that are wrong. He can create desires and passions within us that are so strong we think we must yield to them. But that is a lie, because he is a liar. We do not have to yield to them. He can lure us, he can deceive us. . . . But the great declaration of this Scripture is that once you know Jesus Christ, the devil can never again make you sin.[94]

The Bible assures, "God is faithful; he will not let you be tempted beyond what you can bear. But when you are tempted, he will also provide a way out so that you can stand up under it" (1 Cor. 10:13).

On the night that Satan tried to "repossess" Peter, Jesus said, "Simon, Simon . . . Satan hath desired to have you, that he may sift you as wheat: but I have prayed for thee, that thy faith fail not" (Luke 22:31-32, KJV).

A child explained his conversion: "I heard a knock at the door, and saw it was Jesus. I asked Him to come in. He did. I heard another knock. I said, 'Jesus, You go to the door.' He did, and Satan was there. When he saw Jesus, he said, 'Oh, I've made a mistake. I'm at the wrong place.'"[95]

Fellow believers, our security is not our grasp on Jesus,

but His grasp on us. "In all these things we have complete victory through him who loved us!" (Rom. 8:37, TEV).

III. GOD KEEPS HIS WORD ABOUT BEING SECURE IN HIS FAMILY

Here's John's third ring of certainty: "*We know*."

"We know that we are children of God, and that the whole world is under the control of the evil one" (v. 19).

The believer's new position as a member of God's family is part of the remedy for sin. Being born of God, he belongs to the family.

An irate subscriber stormed into a newspaper office, waving the current edition. He wanted to see the person who wrote the obituary column. Referred to the cub reporter, he stabbed with his finger at the column, which included his obituary. "You can see I am very much alive. I demand a retraction!"

The reporter replied, "We don't retract stories. But I'll tell you what I will do. I'll put you in the birth column and give you a fresh start!"

Every one of us believers were glad for the fresh start of being born into the family of God. With confidence we can declare, "We know that we are children of God."

Stedman says that critics will insist, "What smug presumption. Imagine! That's the trouble with you Christians. You think you're so much better than everyone else. You think you're superior."[96] We're not superior, but we're grateful to God. We *are* a blessed people! We rejoice, but the world reacts because it is "under the control of the evil one." John pictures in the Greek text the world order embraced in the arms of Satan, being morally rocked to sleep. But we belong to Jesus. He will go to any length to protect His own—clear to the Cross itself.

A quaint little highland village lay nestled between barren crags in the rugged Scottish mountains. Many of the villagers were working in the fields while small children played nearby and babies slept in baskets.

Suddenly a huge eagle swooped down and snatched a sleeping infant. With its prey, the eagle perched on a high cliff. Quickly a sailor tried to scale the craggy face, but it was too steep. He gave up. A veteran climber attempted to pick his way, but it was too dangerous. He couldn't make it.

A poor peasant woman risked her life, clutching the sheer rocks. Bravely she edged her way without looking down. While spectators watched in horror, she slowly made her way back down step by step, clutching that rescued baby in her arms. Why did she succeed when the others failed? That woman loved the baby. She had given birth to it. It belonged to her!

An even greater love drove God's Son to Calvary's hill: "For God so loved the world, that he gave his only begotten Son, that whosoever believeth in him should not perish, but have everlasting life" (John 3:16, KJV). Nothing can deprive you of His love. You can do nothing to make God love you less; you can do nothing to make Him love you more. No one can come between you and Him. You belong to His family. Jesus said, "My Father, who has given them to me, is greater than all; no one can snatch them out of my Father's hand" (John 10:29).

IV. GOD KEEPS HIS WORD ABOUT THE RELIABILITY OF JESUS

For the fourth time, John emphasizes, *"We know."*

"We know also that the Son of God has come and has given us understanding, so that we may know him who is true. And we are in him who is true—even in his Son Jesus Christ. He is the true God and eternal life" (v. 20).

The Gnostics, whom John is confronting, believed that God's Son did not come in the flesh. To them anything physical was inherently evil. Therefore, they said, Jesus was only a man, but the Christ, a phantom, merely rested on the man Jesus. The phantom Christ departed before the Crucifixion. Their Christ was not real.

With assurance, John says, "We know also that the Son of God *has come*." John's Gospel was based on the fact that "the Word became flesh and made his dwelling among us" (1:14). It had been 60 years since John first saw Jesus—but it was fresh on his mind. Jesus had given him "an understanding" of God. "We have seen his glory, the glory of the One and Only, who came from the Father, full of grace and truth. . . . No one has ever seen God, but God the One and Only, who is at the Father's side, has made him known" (1:14, 18). More than knowing *about* Him, we know *Him*.

A man traveled a long distance to interview a distinguished scholar. Upon arrival, he was cordially received. Before being seated, he said to his host, "Doctor, I see that the walls of your study are lined with books from ceiling to floor. I know you have written many yourself. You have traveled widely and have no doubt conversed with interesting people. I have come a long way to ask you one question—of all you've learned, what are the things most worth knowing?"

As the scholar put his hand on the guest's shoulder, he replied with a depth of emotion, "Sir, of all the things I have learned, only two are really worth knowing. The first is, I am a great sinner; and the second, Jesus Christ is a great Savior!"

Paul exclaimed: "Christ Jesus came into the world to save sinners—of whom I am the worst" (1 Tim. 1:15).

Like many writers, John adds a postscript. Recognizing the reliability of Jesus, John gives a parting word—and it sounds like a parent shouting a last word of advice as his child is leaving home. In the sequence of chronological time, these are some of the last words written in the Bible: "Dear children, keep yourselves from idols" (v. 21).

John, the last surviving apostle, now an old man, lived in Ephesus. In that city, the temple of Diana was one of the seven wonders of the ancient world. Acts 19 portrays the conflict when Christians came to town. Idol worship of Diana included extremely immoral ceremonies. Awarded the right asylum, the dregs of humanity hovered around the temple precincts. Ephesian craftsmen earned their livelihood by making charms and idols for the pagan world. Such a society put pressure on Christians to conform or compromise. John challenged them, "Keep yourselves from idols."

An idol is a substitute for the real thing. An idol is anything that comes between a person and God. The things people idolize tend to push God into the margins of life.

Ancient temples of the old Greek and Roman world are abandoned, but the worship of the gods have not ceased: "We have changed the names, but the gods, the idols, are exactly the same . . . worship of Narcissus, the god who fell in love with himself . . . worship of Bacchus, the god of pleasure, the god of wine, women and song . . . worship of Venus, the goddess of love . . . Apollo, the god of physical beauty . . . Minerva, the goddess of science."[97]

Carl F. H. Henry warned, "Although modern man zestfully explores outer space, he seems quite content to live in a spiritual kindergarten and to play in a moral wilderness." He actually plays with gods of his own making. The Bible warns, "Those who make them will be like them, and so will all who trust in them" (Ps. 115:8). We become like what we worship. One man commented, *"The thing we serve is the thing we worship!* Whatever controls our lives and 'calls the signals' is our god."⁹⁸

Assured of the reality and reliability of Jesus, John calls out, "Dear children, keep away from anything that might take God's place in your hearts" (TLB).

Phil was an associate of Christian psychologist Clyde Narramore. One day, around the lunch table, Phil confided, "I have to confess—I don't know if I'm really saved or not."

One of the fellows asked, "What do you mean?"

Phil replied, "I've gone to church all my life. I've taught classes. I served as superintendent of the Sunday School. But I can't say for sure that I'm saved. I hear you men talk as if you know definitely that you are saved— and that disturbs me! I don't have that assurance."

Dr. Narramore began reading from 1 John 5:12—"He who has the Son has life; he who does not have the Son of God does not have life."

Phil said, "I never knew that was in the Bible."

Going on to the next verse, Dr. Narramore read aloud, "I write these things to you who believe in the name of the Son of God so that you may know that you have eternal life" (v. 13).

They went over that verse several times. Dr. Narramore said, "Phil, I see two important things in this verse. One is the fact that God has given us this written Word in order for us to believe on His name. The second fact is that He has given us the written Word so that after we believe on His name, we can know for sure that we have eternal life. Believe and know—God doesn't want us uncertain about it. He says in His own Word that we can be saved and know for sure."

Eagerly, Phil said, "Since I actually don't know

whether I'm saved or not, I'd like to make sure right now." He quietly bowed his head and prayed simply, "Lord, come into my heart and save me. If I have never before given my life to You, I am doing so right now. Please forgive me of my sins—and be my Lord. And thank You for doing it. In Jesus' name I pray. Amen."

What a precious moment it was! From then on Phil was certain, not because of his feelings, but because God's Word said so—and God keeps His Word. A great change came in Phil's life as he began to grow spiritually.

Months later, Dr. Narramore asked Phil if he still had his "know-so" salvation. "Of course I do," Phil said. "Since that day around the lunch table when I settled it all, I've never had any doubt in my mind."

"But how can you be sure?" Dr. Narramore questioned.

"Because God says so in His Word—and God keeps His Word."[99]

Nothing is more dependable than God's Word. Jesus said, "Heaven and earth will pass away, but my words will never pass away" (Matt. 24:35).

Notes

Preface
*T. W. Willingham, *Crumbs for the Tested/Growing Christians: Spiritual Insights of T. W. Willingham*, book 3 (Kansas City: Beacon Hill Press of Kansas City, 1987), 29.

Chapter 1
1. E. M. Blaiklock, *Letters to Children of Light* (Glendale, Calif.: Regal Books, 1975), 8.
2. Reuben Welch, *We Really Do Need Each Other* (Nashville: Impact Books, a division of John T. Benson Publishing Co., n.d.), 26.
3. Ibid., 27.
4. Warren W. Wiersbe, *Be Real* (Wheaton, Ill.: Victor Books, a division of SP Publications, 1980), 20-21.

Chapter 2
5. Donald W. Burdick, *The Epistles of John* (Chicago: Moody Press, 1970), 25.
6. Ray C. Stedman, *Life by the Son* (Waco, Tex.: Word Books, Publisher, 1980), 33.
7. Ibid.
8. Ibid., 34.
9. Ibid.
10. Ibid., 35.
11. Ibid.
12. Ibid., 35-36.
13. Wiersbe, *Be Real*, 45-46.
14. T. W. Willingham, *A Second Basket of Crumbs* (Kansas City: Beacon Hill Press of Kansas City, 1975), 21.
15. H. A. Ironside, *Addresses on the Epistles of John and an Exposition of the Epistle of Jude* (Neptune, N.J.: Loizeaux Brothers, 1931), 28.
16. Nelda Bishop Reed, in an unidentified article in *Come Ye Apart*, n.d.
17. Wiersbe, *Be Real*, 15.
18. Nelson G. Mink, *That Ye Sin Not* (Kansas City: Beacon Hill Press of Kansas City, 1969), 19.

Chapter 3
19. Welch, *We Really Do Need Each Other*, 52.
20. Stedman, *Life by the Son*, 52-53.
21. Alice J. Hall, "Buffalo Bill and the Enduring West," *National Geographic* 160, no. 1 (July 1981): 91.
22. Reuben Welch, *To Timothy and All Other Disciples* (Kansas City: Beacon Hill Press of Kansas City, 1979), 57.
23. D. Shelby Corlett, *God in the Present Tense* (Kansas City: Beacon Hill Press of Kansas City, 1974), 43.
24. Stedman, *Life by the Son*, 49.

Chapter 4

25. William McCumber, "To Keep from Backsliding," *Herald of Holiness*, Apr. 15, 1981, 19.

26. Stedman, *Life by the Son*, 54.

27. Robert Shank, *Life in the Son* (Springfield, Mo.: Westcott Publishers, 1960), 135.

28. Welch, *We Really Do Need Each Other*, 61.

29. Ibid., 62.

30. Ibid., 64.

31. Ironside, *Epistles of John*, 45-46.

32. W. T. Purkiser, "Provision, Not Allowance," *Herald of Holiness*, Feb. 16, 1972.

33. Ibid.

Chapter 5

34. Augustine, *Confessions of St. Augustine*, 397, quoted in Ralph L. Woods, comp. and ed., *The World Treasury of Religious Quotations* (New York: Garland Books, 1966), 853.

35. James Montgomery Boice, *The Epistles of John* (Grand Rapids: Wm. B. Eerdmans Publishing Co., 1978), 56-57.

36. Stedman, *Life by the Son*, 65.

37. Blaiklock, *Letters to Children of Light*, 34.

38. Stedman, *Life by the Son*, 66.

39. Wiersbe, *Be Real*, 61.

40. Stedman, *Life by the Son*, 72-73.

Chapter 6

41. Lloyd John Ogilvie, *When God First Thought of You* (Waco, Tex.: Word Books, Publisher, 1978), 46.

42. Stedman, *Life by the Son*, 101.

43. Ibid., 103-4.

44. Ibid., 106.

45. Wiersbe, *Be Real*, 74-75.

46. Ibid., 78.

Chapter 7

47. Stedman, *Life by the Son*, 120.

48. Anthony A. Hoekema, *The Four Major Cults* (n.p., n.d.), 375.

49. Ironside, *Epistles of John*, 80-81.

50. Wiersbe, *Be Real*, 92.

51. Stedman, *Life by the Son*, 128-29.

52. Ogilvie, *When God First Thought of You*, 62.

53. Ibid., 61-62.

54. Ibid., 62.

55. Ibid.

56. Charles W. Colson, *Born Again* (Old Tappan, N.J.: Chosen Books, 1976), 127.

Chapter 8

57. *Pulpit Resource* 9, no. 4 (October—December 1981).

58. Ironside, *Epistles of John*, 87-88.

59. Wiersbe, *Be Real*, 94.

60. John T. Seamands, *Tell It Well: Communicating the Gospel Across Cultures* (Kansas City: Beacon Hill Press of Kansas City, 1981), 69.

61. Ibid., 60.

62. Stedman, *Life by the Son*, 132.

63. Ibid., 154.

64. Ibid., 154-55.

Chapter 9

65. Wiersbe, *Be Real*, 105.

Chapter 10

66. Erwin W. Lutzer, *Failure: The Back Door to Success* (Chicago: Moody Press, 1975), 93-94.

Chapter 11

67. Welch, *We Really Do Need Each Other*, 70-72.

68. William Barclay, *The Letters of John and Jude*, in *The Daily Study Bible Series* (Philadelphia: Westminster Press, 1960), 100.

Chapter 12

69. Stedman, *Life by the Son*, 282.

70. Wiersbe, *Be Real*, 133.

Chapter 13

71. Stedman, *Life by the Son*, 297.

72. Ibid.

73. Blaiklock, *Letters to Children of Light*, 77.

74. From an unidentified source in *Reader's Digest*, June 1969.

75. Anthony Campolo, "The All-American God—Have We Made God into Our Own Image?" *These Times*, March 1980.

76. Burdick, *The Epistles of John*.

77. E. Stanley Jones, *The Christ of the Indian Road* (New York: Abingdon Press, 1925), 163.

78. Ibid.

79. C. S. Lewis, *Mere Christianity* (New York: Macmillan Co., 1960), 40-41.

Chapter 14

80. Wiersbe, *Be Real*, 152.

81. Ibid., 145-46.

82. Stedman, *Life by the Son*, 322.

83. Wiersbe, *Be Real*, 150.

Chapter 15

84. E. Stanley Jones, *In Christ* (New York: Abingdon Press, 1961), 354.

85. Mink, *That Ye Sin Not*, 54-55.

86. W. T. Purkiser, *Exploring Christian Holiness, Vol. 1* (Kansas City: Beacon Hill Press of Kansas City, 1983), 85.

87. David A. Seamands, *Putting Away Childish Things* (Wheaton, Ill.: Victor Books, a division of SP Publications, 1982), 94.

88. Wiersbe, *Be Real*, 157.

89. Welch, *We Really Do Need Each Other*, 107-9.

Chapter 16

90. Wiersbe, *Be Real*, 165.

91. Ibid., 169-70.

Chapter 17

92. Norman Vincent Peale, *The Positive Power of Jesus Christ* (Pawling, N.Y.: Foundation for Christian Living, 1980), 143-46.

93. Barclay, *Letters of John and Jude*, 138.

94. Stedman, *Life by the Son*, 374.

95. E. Stanley Jones, *The Way* (Garden City, N.Y.: Doubleday and Co., 1978), 88.

96. Stedman, *Life by the Son*, 375.

97. Ibid., 380.

98. Wiersbe, *Be Real*, 188.

99. Clyde M. Narramore, *This Way to Happiness* (Grand Rapids: Zondervan Publishing House, 1958), 177-78.

Bibliography

Allen, Charles L. *Healing Words*. Westwood, N.J.: Fleming H. Revell Co., 1961.
Angell, C. Roy. *Shields of Brass*. Nashville: Broadman Press, 1965.
Barclay, William. *The Letters of John and Jude*. In *The Daily Study Bible Series*. Philadelphia: Westminster Press, 1960.
Blaiklock, E. M. *Letters to Children of Light*. Glendale, Calif.: Regal Books, a division of G/L Publications, 1975.
Boice, James Montgomery. *The Epistles of John*. Grand Rapids: Wm. B. Eerdmans Publishing Co., 1978.
Burdick, Donald W. *The Epistles of John*. Chicago: Moody Press, 1970.
Clarke, Adam. *Clarke's Commentary*, vol. 6. New York: Abingdon Press, n.d.
Colson, Charles W. *Born Again*. Old Tappan, N.J.: Chosen Books, 1976.
Cook, Jerry. *Love, Acceptance, and Forgiveness*. Glendale, Calif.: Regal Books, 1979.
Corlett, D. Shelby. *God in the Present Tense*. Kansas City: Beacon Hill Press of Kansas City, 1974.
Hall, Alice J. "Buffalo Bill and the Enduring West." *National Geographic* 160, no. 1 (July 1981): 91.
Hoekema, Anthony A. *The Four Major Cults*. N.p., n.d.
Ironside, H. A. *Addresses on the Epistles of John and an Exposition of the Epistle of Jude*. Neptune, N.J.: Loizeaux Brothers, 1931.
Jones, E. Stanley. *In Christ*. New York: Abingdon Press, 1961.
———. *The Way*. Garden City, N.Y.: Doubleday and Co., 1978.
Kivengere, Bishop Festo. *Love Unlimited*. Glendale, Calif.: Regal Books, 1975.
Lutzer, Erwin W. *Failure: The Back Door to Success*. Chicago: Moody Press, 1975.
Mink, Nelson G. *That Ye Sin Not*. Kansas City: Beacon Hill Press of Kansas City, 1969.
Narramore, Clyde M. *This Way to Happiness*. Grand Rapids: Zondervan Publishing House, 1958.
Ogilvie, Lloyd John. *When God First Thought of You*. Waco, Tex.: Word Books, Publisher, 1978.
Palmer, Earl F. *The Communicator's Commentary*, vol. 12. Edited by Lloyd John Ogilvie. Waco, Tex.: Word Books, Publisher, 1982.
Purkiser, W. T. *Exploring Christian Holiness*, vol. 1, *The Biblical Foundations*. Kansas City: Beacon Hill Press of Kansas City, 1983.
Robertson, Archibald Thomas. *Word Pictures in the New Testament*, vol. 6. Nashville: Broadman Press, 1933.
Seamands, David A. *Putting Away Childish Things*. Wheaton, Ill.: Victor Books, a division of SP Publications, 1982.
Seamands, John T. *Tell It Well: Communicating the Gospel Across Cultures*. Kansas City: Beacon Hill Press of Kansas City, 1981.
Shank, Robert. *Life in the Son*. Springfield, Mo.: Westcott Publishers, 1960.
Stedman, Ray C. *Life by the Son*. Waco, Tex.: Word Books, Publisher, 1980.
Stott, John R. W. *The Epistles of John*, Vol. 19 of *Tyndale Bible Commentaries*. Grand Rapids: Wm. B. Eerdmans Publishing Co., 1964.

Welch, Reuben. *To Timothy and All Other Disciples*. Kansas City: Beacon Hill Press of Kansas City, 1979.

———. *We Really Do Need Each Other*. Nashville: Impact Books, a division of John T. Benson Publishing Co., n.d.

Wiersbe, Warren W. *Be Real*. Wheaton, Ill.: Victor Books, 1980.

Willingham, T. W. *Crumbs for the Tested/Growing Christian: Spiritual Insights of T. W. Willingham*, book 3. Kansas City: Beacon Hill Press of Kansas City, 1987.

———. *A Second Basket of Crumbs*. Kansas City: Beacon Hill Press of Kansas City, 1975.

Wynkoop, Mildred Bangs. *A Theology of Love*. Kansas City: Beacon Hill Press of Kansas City, 1972.